KÖNEMANN

© 2015 for this edition: koenemann.com GmbH

Distributed in cooperation with Frechmann Kolón GmbH

www.koenemann.com

www.frechmann.com

Published in the United States in 2016 by:

Skyhorse Publishing

307 West 36th Street, 11th Floor

New York, NY 10018, USA

T: +1 212 643 6816

info@skyhorsepublishing.com

www.skyhorsepublishing.com

Editorial project: LOFT Publications

Barcelona, Spain

Tel.: +34 932 688 088

Fax: +34 932 687 073

loft@loftpublications.com

www.loftpublications.com

Editorial coordinator: Claudia Martínez Alonso

Assistant to editorial coordination: Ana Marques

Art director: Mireia Casanovas Soley

Edition and texts: Àlex Sánchez Vidiella

Layout: Cristina Simó Perales

Layout assistant: Kseniya Palvinskaya

Translations: Textcase

ISBN 978-3-86407-289-5 (GB)

ISBN 978-3-86407-287-1 (D)

ISBN 978-3-86407-288-8 (E)

ISBN 978-1-5107-0453-4 (Skyhorse, USA)

Printed in Spain

Wood is one of the best materials for construction on account of its versatility. Among other benefits, its outstanding features are its great capacity as a thermal and acoustic insulator; its remarkable ecological character; warm appearance; luminosity, and comfort, as well as its pleasant texture and feel. For these reasons, architects and designers use this noble material, which offers infinite possibilities for exterior design and decoration. Today, the new criteria for sustainable housing planning benefit from an inexhaustible source of ideas based on products derived from this material. Furthermore, the great variety of available wood, and the fact that it is easy to recycle, facilitate the construction of masterful and varied designs. New ways of joining and fixing have been formulated thanks to modern technology.

The contact with nature that this material affords has successfully revitalized the use of wood in domestic architecture. In this sense, the clients who request these types of housing do so because they believe in the benefits that wood brings to their lives, satisfying their tastes, their requirements, and their individual lifestyles. This type of client requires energy efficiency, modern construction technologies, rapid assembly times and lower costs. Wooden houses can be perfectly adapted to the required functionality and aesthetic tastes of the people who choose them.

This book is a compilation of different types of construction—second homes, pre-fabricated houses, cabins, retreats, nurseries, cafés, etc., which unify traditional design with different styles of modern and contemporary creations. Retirement homes provide examples of harmony between the traditional and the modern; contemporary dwellings show a reinterpretation of typical wood cabins; simple houses show austerity of design; pre-fabricated homes reflect cost and energy saving in their construction; urban or suburban homes are effective examples of adaptation to previously difficult terrain; nurseries show the beneficial use of wood for the little ones, and finally, small delicatessens demonstrate the amazing wonders that can be constructed from wood.

The Canadian, Central European, Mediterranean, Northern European, and above all, Asian examples are displayed in large-scale images and detailed plans. Focused on the use of wood, the explanatory texts clearly explain the characteristics of this material and its use in sophisticated residences and contemporary homes.

En raison de sa diversité et de son vaste champ d'application, le bois est l'un des meilleurs matériaux de construction. Parmi ses atouts, on peut citer sa grande capacité d'isolation thermique et acoustique, son caractère écologique évident, son aspect chaleureux, sa luminosité, son confort ainsi que sa texture et son toucher agréables. Les architectes et designers d'aujourd'hui utilisent ce matériau noble parce qu'il offre d'innombrables possibilités en termes de design extérieur et de décoration. Les produits dérivés de ce matériau leur offrent une source inépuisable d'idées pour leurs projets fondés sur la durabilité. De plus, la grande variété de bois et son recyclage aisé permettent la construction de magnifiques réalisations variées. Grâce à la technologie, de nouveaux traitements du bois ont pu être créés afin de le conserver et de l'entretenir, ainsi que de nouveaux systèmes de jonction et de fixation. Le contact avec la nature qu'offre ce matériau a fait renaître l'utilisation du bois dans l'architecture domestique.

Les clients demandent ce type d'habitations parce qu'ils croient aux avantages que le bois apporte à leur vie ; il répond à leurs goûts, à leurs besoins et à leur style de vie. L'efficacité énergétique, les technologies modernes de construction, le délai de fabrication rapide et la diminution des coûts sont les exigences invoquées par ces clients. Les maisons en bois peuvent parfaitement s'adapter à la fonctionnalité et au goût esthétique des personnes qui envisagent de les utiliser.

Ce livre est un recueil des différentes typologies de construction – résidences secondaires, maisons préfabriquées, cabanes, refuges, crèches, cafés, etc. – qui allient le design traditionnel aux créations modernes et contemporaines de différents styles. Ainsi, les maisons de retraite sont des exemples d'harmonie entre tradition et modernité ; les maisons modernes réinterprètent des cabanes en bois caractéristiques ; les maisons simples sont de conception austère ; les maisons préfabriquées reflètent l'économie énergétique et la diminution des coûts de construction ; les maisons urbaines ou de banlieue sont des exemples réels de l'adaptation à des terrains a priori difficiles ; les crèches montrent l'utilisation bénéfique du bois pour les plus petits ; et enfin, les petites réalisations illustrent les merveilles surprenantes que le bois a permis de construire.

Les projets canadiens, d'Europe centrale, méditerranéens, d'Europe du Nord et surtout asiatiques sont présentés dans un grand format et des plans détaillés. La clarté des textes explicatifs, consacrés à l'utilisation du bois, permet de comprendre les caractéristiques de ce matériau utilisé dans des résidences sophistiquées et des foyers contemporains.

Aufgrund seiner Vielseitigkeit ist Holz eines der besten Materialien für den Möbelbau. Neben anderen Vorteilen hebt es sich besonders durch seine Fähigkeit als Wärme- und Schalldämmstoff ab, sowie durch seine markanten ökologischen Eigenschaften, das warme Erscheinungsbild, seine Leuchtkraft, seine Behaglichkeit und durch seine angenehme Struktur und Haptik. Aus diesen Gründen verwenden Architekten und Designer dieses edle Material, da es unendlich viele Möglichkeiten für die Gestaltung von Außenanlagen und für die Dekoration bietet. Heutzutage haben die neuen Kriterien bei der Planung des Wohnungsbaus, die auf Nachhaltigkeit beruhen, in den Produkten, die aus diesem Material entstanden sind, eine unerschöpfliche Quelle von Ideen gefunden. Außerdem erlauben die große Vielzahl an Holzsorten und ihr einfaches Recycling die Konstruktion virtuoser und abwechslungsreicher Muster. Die Technik hat dazu beigetragen, neue Behandlungsmethoden für Holz hervorzubringen, damit es richtig konserviert und unterhalten wird, sowie neue Systeme für die Verbindung und Befestigung zu entwickeln. Der Kontakt mit der Natur, den dieses Material vermittelt, hat dazu geführt, dass die Verwendung von Holz in der Hausarchitektur einen neuen Aufschwung erlebt hat.

Den Kontakt zur Natur suchen auch die Kunden, die diese Art von Wohnhäusern wünschen, sie glauben an die Vorteile von Holz für ihr Leben sowie daran dass es ihren jeweiligen Geschmack, ihre Bedürfnisse und ihre speziellen Lebensstile befriedigt. Energetische Effizienz, moderne Technologien beim Bau, ein kurzer Zeitrahmen bei der Herstellung und geringere Kosten, sind Anforderungen, die diese Kunden stellen. Die Holzhäuser passen sich perfekt an die Funktionalität und den ästhetischen Geschmack der Personen an, die sie nutzen möchten.

Dieses Buch ist eine Zusammenstellung der verschiedenen Bautypen, wie beispielsweise Zweitwohnsitze, Fertighäuser, Blockhütten, Unterstände, Kindertagesstätten, Cafés, usw., die traditionelles Design mit modernen und zeitgenössischen Kreationen verschiedener Stile vereinen. Altenheime sind ein Beispiel für die Harmonie zwischen Tradition und modernem Stil; zeitgenössische Wohnhäuser zeigen eine Neuinterpretation der typischen Holzblockhütten; einfache Häuser bieten ihr Design eine gewisse Nüchternheit; Fertighäuser spiegeln Themen wie Energieeinsparung und Reduzierung der Konstruktionskosten wider; Stadthäuser oder Häuser in den Vorstädten sind effektive Beispiele für die Anpassung an Bodenbeschaffenheiten, die a priori schwierig sind; Kindertagesstätten repräsentieren den praktischen Nutzen von Holz für die Kleinsten; schließlich zeigen die kleinen „Delikatessen" die erstaunlichen Wunder, die aus Holz erschaffen werden konnten.

Die Vorschläge aus Kanada, Mitteleuropa, dem Mittelmeerraum, Nordeuropa und vor allem aus Asien werden anhand von großformatigen Bilder und detaillierten Plänen dargestellt. Die deutlichen Texte, in denen es um die Nutzung von Holzes geht, helfen dabei, eine optimale Erklärung über die Eigenschaften des Materials zu bieten, das in hochentwickelten Wohnhäusern und zeitgenössischen Wohnstätten verwendet wird.

Hout heeft ruime toepassingsmogelijkheden en is daardoor een van de beste constructiematerialen. Het heeft enorm veel goede eigenschappen. Zo is het onder meer bijzonder geschikt als thermisch en akoestisch isolatiemateriaal, heeft het uitgesproken ecologische voordelen en een warme en heldere uitstraling. Het is comfortabel, heeft een aangename structuur en voelt prettig aan. Om al deze redenen maken architecten en ontwerpers graag gebruik van dit hoogstaande materiaal. Hout biedt oneindig veel ontwerp- en decoratiemogelijkheden, zowel voor buiten als binnen. Met alle nieuwe eisen die binnen de woningbouw worden gesteld aan duurzaamheid, bieden hout en alle afgeleiden daarvan een onuitputtelijke bron van mogelijkheden. Omdat er zo veel soorten hout bestaan en het eenvoudig hergebruikt kan worden, kunnen er bovendien heel verschillende en zeer creatieve voorbeelden mee worden gebouwd. Door de technische vooruitgang zijn er niet alleen nieuwe bewerkingen mogelijk, waardoor hout beter geconserveerd en onderhouden kan worden, maar zijn er ook nieuwe methoden ontdekt om hout te verbinden en te bevestigen. Er wordt ook steeds meer hout toegepast binnen de huizenbouw, omdat het mensen in contact brengt met de natuur.

Mensen die graag in dit soort huizen wonen, doen dat dan ook omdat ze geloven dat hout een positieve invloed heeft op hun leven, omdat ze het materiaal mooi vinden, dat het voorziet in hun behoeften en aansluit bij hun specifieke levensstijl. Het zijn mensen die vragen om efficiënt energiegebruik, moderne bouwtechnieken, een snelle productietermijn en lagere kosten. Houten huizen kunnen perfect worden aangepast aan wat de mensen die erin willen wonen nodig hebben en mooi vinden.

Dit boek bevat een verzameling van zeer uiteenlopende bouwwerken. Er staan vakantiewoningen en prefab huizen in, maar ook hutten, tijdelijke onderkomens, kinderdagverblijven, cafés en meer. Het is een bundeling van traditionele ontwerpen en moderne en eigentijdse creaties in allerlei stijlen. Sommige toevluchtsoorden zijn een goed voorbeeld van een harmonieus samengaan van traditionele bouwstijlen met moderne creaties. Veel eigentijdse woningen laten zien dat een nieuwe interpretatie mogelijk is van de typisch houten hutten. Er zijn prachtige sobere ontwerpen van eenvoudige huizen, prefabhuizen die een toonbeeld zijn van hoe er bespaard kan worden op energie en bouwkosten, huizen in (voor)steden waarmee doeltreffend wordt aangetoond dat het met aanpassingen mogelijk is op terreinen te bouwen die a priori niet geschikt voor lijken te zijn, crèches die getuigen van de positieve invloed van het gebruik van hout op de allerkleinsten, en allerlei verrassende ontwerpen die laten zien welke prachtige dingen er gebouwd kunnen worden van hout.

Naast de grote foto's en gedetailleerde tekeningen van de diverse ontwerpen van geavanceerde gebouwen en eigentijdse huizen in Canada, Midden-, Zuid- en Noord-Europa en met name in Azië wordt in heldere bewoordingen zo uitgebreid mogelijk uiteengezet wat de specifieke eigenschappen van hout zijn.

La madera constituye uno de los mejores materiales para la construcción debido a su versatilidad. Entre otros beneficios, destaca su gran capacidad como aislante térmico y acústico, su marcado carácter ecológico, su aspecto cálido, su luminosidad, su confort y su agradable textura. Por estos motivos, los arquitectos y diseñadores utilizan este material noble porque proporciona unas posibilidades de diseño exterior y decoración infinitas. En la actualidad, los nuevos criterios en la planificación de viviendas basados en la sostenibilidad han encontrado una fuente inagotable de ideas en los productos derivados de este material. Además, la gran variedad de madera y el reciclaje de la misma permiten la construcción de virtuosas y variadas muestras. La tecnología ha servido para crear nuevos tratamientos de la madera para una correcta conservación y manutención de la misma, así como nuevos sistemas de unión y fijación.

El contacto con la naturaleza que proporciona este material ha hecho renacer en el uso de la madera en la arquitectura doméstica. En este sentido, los clientes que demandan este tipo de viviendas lo hacen porque cree en los beneficios que la madera aporta a sus vidas, satisfacen sus gustos, sus necesidades y sus particulares estilos de vida. La eficiencia energética, las tecnologías modernas en la construcción, unos tiempos de fabricación breves y un abaratamiento en los costes son los requisitos que este tipo de clientes precisan. Las casas de madera pueden adaptarse perfectamente a la funcionalidad y el gusto estético de las personas que piensan utilizarlas.

Este libro es una recopilación de diferentes tipologías constructivas tales como segundas residencias, casas prefabricadas, cabañas, refugios, guarderías, cafés, etc., que aúnan diseño tradicional con modernas y contemporáneas creaciones de diferentes estilos. Así pues, las casas de retiro son ejemplos de armonía entre lo tradicional y lo moderno; los hogares contemporáneos muestran una reinterpretación de las típicas cabañas de madera; las casas sencillas presentan la austeridad en sus diseños; las prefabricadas son reflejos del ahorro energético y de costes en la construcción; las casas urbanas o suburbanas son efectivos ejemplos de la adaptación a terrenos difíciles a priori; las guarderías presentan el uso beneficioso de la madera para los más pequeños; y, finalmente, pequeñas delicias muestran sorprendentes virguerías que la madera ha permitido construir.

Las propuestas canadienses, centroeuropeas, mediterráneas, norteeuropeas y, sobre todo, asiáticas se mostradas a través de imágenes de gran formato y planos detallados. La claridad de los textos explicativos centrados en la utilización de la madera ayuda a lograr una óptima descripción de las características de este material empleado en sofisticadas residencias y hogares contemporáneos.

Il legno rappresenta uno dei materiali migliori per costruire grazie alla sua versatilità. Tra le varie qualità spicca la sua grande capacità di isolamento termico e acustico, il marcato carattere ecologico, l'aspetto caldo, la luminosità, il comfort e la piacevole venatura e sensazione al tatto. Per tutte queste ragioni, gli architetti e i designer utilizzano questo nobile materiale perché offre possibilità infinite per il design d'esterni e l'arredamento. Attualmente, i nuovi criteri nella progettazione di spazi abitativi che si basano sulla sostenibilità hanno trovato nei prodotti derivati da questo materiale una fonte inesauribile di idee. Inoltre, la grande varietà di legni e il loro facile riciclaggio consentono la costruzione di svariati e virtuosi modelli. La tecnologia è stata utile a creare nuovi trattamenti del legno per la sua corretta conservazione e manutenzione, così come nuovi sistemi di saldatura e fissaggio.

Il contatto con la natura che questo materiale offre ha fatto rivivere l'utilizzo del legno nell'architettura domestica. In questo senso, i clienti che richiedono questo tipo di abitazioni lo fanno perché credono nei benefici che il legno apporta alle loro vite, soddisfa i loro gusti, i loro bisogni e i loro particolari stili di vita. L'efficienza energetica, le moderne tecnologie della costruzione, dei tempi rapidi di fabbricazione e una riduzione dei costi, rappresentano i requisiti necessari per questi clienti. Le case di legno sono in grado di adattarsi perfettamente alla funzionalità e al gusto estetico delle persone che intendono utilizzarle.

Questo libro è una raccolta di differenti tipologie costruttive, come seconde case, case prefabbricate, capanne, rifugi, asili nido, caffè, etc., che uniscono la progettazione tradizionale con creazioni moderne e contemporanee di vari stili. Così, le case di riposo sono un esempio di armonia tra tradizione e modernità; le dimore contemporanee mostrano una rilettura delle tipiche capanne di legno; le case semplici denotano austerità nel loro design; quelle prefabbricate sono un riflesso del risparmio di energia e di costi di costruzione; le case cittadine o periferiche sono esempi efficienti dell'adattamento a terreni difficili; gli asili nido presentano un utilizzo efficace del legno per i più piccoli; e, infine, le piccole delicatessen rivelano le sorprendenti meraviglie che il legno ha permesso di costruire.

Le proposte canadesi, centro-europee, mediterranee, nordeuropee e, soprattutto, asiatiche sono presentate attraverso immagini di grandi dimensioni e piantine dettagliate. La chiarezza dei testi esplicativi, concentrati sull'utilizzo del legno, permette di avere un'ottima spiegazione delle caratteristiche di questo materiale impiegato in residenze raffinate e case contemporanee.

Graças à sua versatilidade, a madeira constitui um dos melhores materiais para construção. Entre outras vantagens, é muito eficiente como isolante térmico e acústico, tem um vincado caráter ecológico e um aspecto quente e luminoso, transmite uma sensação de conforto e a sua textura é agradável ao tato. Por todos estes motivos, os arquitetos e designers utilizam frequentemente este material tão nobre, que oferece um vasto leque de possibilidades em arquitetura, tanto de exteriores como de interiores. Atualmente, os novos critérios para conceção de habitações, com especial enfoque na sustentabilidade, encontraram nos derivados deste material uma fonte inesgotável de inspiração. Além disso, a enorme variedade de madeiras existente e a sua fácil reciclagem permitem a criação de variadíssimas propostas. Os avanços tecnológicos possibilitaram a criação de novos tratamentos para a madeira, permitindo a sua correta conservação e manutenção, assim como novos sistemas de união e fixação.

O contato com a natureza proporcionado por este material determinou também a recuperação do uso da madeira na arquitetura doméstica. Deste modo, os clientes que procuram este tipo de casas fazem-no porque acreditam nos benefícios que a madeira lhes pode trazer, satisfazendo os seus gostos, as suas necessidades e os seus estilos de vida particulares. Eficiência energética, novas tecnologias de construção, rapidez de execução e redução dos custos são os requisitos que este tipo de clientes quer ver satisfeitos. As casas de madeira podem adaptar-se perfeitamente à funcionalidade e resultado estético pretendidos pelas pessoas que pensam utilizá-las.

Este livro apresenta uma resenha de diferentes tipologias de construção, como casas de férias, casas pré-fabricadas, cabanas, abrigos, jardins de infância, cafés, etc., que combinam as formas tradicionais com criações modernas e contemporâneas de diferentes estilos. Assim, os lares de idosos são exemplos de harmonia entre o tradicional e o moderno; as casas contemporâneas constituem uma reinterpretação das típicas cananas de madeira; as vivendas apresentam formas austeras; as pré-fabricadas refletem a poupança energética e nos custos de construção; as casas urbanas ou suburbanas são exemplos significativos de adaptação a terrenos à partida difíceis; os jardins de infância testemunham os benefícios do uso da madeira pelos mais pequenos; e, finalmente, las pequenas delicatessen ilustram as surpreendentes maravilhas que a madeira permite construir.

As propostas canadianas, centro-europeias, mediterrânicas, norte-europeias e, sobretudo, asiáticas são apresentadas em imagens de grande formato e planos pormenorizados. A clareza dos textos explicativos, centrados na utilização da madeira, contribui para a perfeita compreensão das caraterísticas deste material utilizado em sofisticadas residências e lares contemporâneos.

Trä är ett av de bästa materialen för byggande på grund av dess mångsidighet. Andra fördelar är till exempel dess goda värme- och ljudisolering, dess utmärkande ekologiska egenskaper, dess varma yttre, lyskraft, bekvämlighet och behagliga struktur och känsla. Av dessa skäl använder arkitekter och formgivare detta ädla material eftersom det erbjuder oändliga möjligheter till utvändig design och dekoration. Idag när kriterierna för bostadsbyggande bygger på frågor om hållbarhet har man i de produkter som bygger på trä hittat en outsinlig källa till idéer. Dessutom möjliggör den stora mångfalden av trä och dess enkla återanvändning att briljanta och varierande exemplar konstrueras. Tekniken har bidragit till att skapa nya behandlingar av trä för bättre bevarande och underhåll, samt nya system för hopfogning och fastsättning. Naturkontakten som detta material ger har lyckats med att återuppliva användningen av trä i arkitektur för hus och hem.

Kunder som frågar efter denna typ av bostäder, gör det med andra ord för att de tror på de fördelar som trä tillför deras liv, smak, behov och enskilda livsstilar. Framförallt ställer den här typen av kunder krav på energieffektivitet, modern konstruktionsteknik, en snabb tillverkningstid och en sänkning av kostnaderna.. Trähus kan anpassas perfekt efter den funktionalitet och estetik som de som tänker använda dem efterfrågar.

Den här boken är en sammanställning av olika byggnadstypologier, som fritidshus, prefabricerade hus, stugor, härbärgen, daghem, kaféer, m.fl., som sammanför traditionell design med moderna och samtida skapelser av olika stilar. Således är husen för en lugn och avskild plats ämnad i harmoni mellan det traditionella och det moderna.De samtida hemmen är exempel på en omtolkning av typiska trästugor och de enkla husen är strama i sin design. De prefabricerade husen återspeglar hushållande av energi- och konstuktionskostnader och stads- och förortsbebyggelsen är tydliga exempel på anpassning till svåra terränger. Daghemmen visar upp en nyttig användning av trä för barn. Slutligen, är de små deli-butikerna exempel på de fantastiska underverk som det är möjligt att bygga i trä.

Förslagen från Kanada och länder i Central- samt Nordeuropa, kring Medelhavet och framför allt i Asien visas genom bilder i stora format och detaljerade ritningar. De tydligt förklarade texterna, som fokuserar på träanvändning, bidrar till att uppnå en optimal förklaring till det som kännetecknar detta material som används i exklusiva villor och samtida hem.

RESIDENTIAL INTERIORS

INTÉRIEURS RÉSIDENTIELS

INNENAUSSTATTUNG VON WOHNHÄUSERN

WOONINTERIEURS

INTERIORES RESIDENCIALES

INTERNI AD USO ABITATIVO

INTERIORES RESIDENCIAIS

BOSTADSINTERIÖRER

CEILING UNDER
DAYLIGHT HOUSE

YOKOHAMA, JAPAN
TAKESHI HOSAKA ARCHITECTS
www.hosakatakeshi.com | © Koji Fujii

The project is destined for a couple with children who requested natural light. The property comprises one bedroom, nursery, study, dining room and kitchen. The structure emphasizes the ceiling grille, which covers all the rooms of the house. Larch wood has been used on most surfaces, as it has a comfortable feel.

Le projet est destiné à un couple avec enfants qui demandait de la lumière naturelle. La maison se compose d'une chambre, d'une chambre d'enfants, d'un bureau, d'une salle à manger et d'une cuisine. On distingue la structure grillagée du toit qui englobe les habitacles de la maison. Le mélèze a été largement utilisé afin d'apporter une sensation de confort à l'ensemble.

Das Projekt war für eine Familie mit Kindern gedacht, die sich viel Tageslicht in den Räumen wünschte. Das Wohnhaus setzt sich aus einem Schlafzimmer, Kinderzimmer, Arbeitszimmer, Esszimmer und Küche zusammen. Auffallend ist die Gitterstruktur des Daches, die alle Räume des Hauses umfasst. Für die meisten Oberflächen wurde Lerchenholz verwendet, da es dem Gesamtbild Komfort verleiht.

Dit huis is gebouwd voor een gezin met kinderen dat vroeg om natuurlijk licht. Het gebouw bestaat uit een slaapkamer voor de ouders, een kinderkamer, werkplaats, eetkamer en keuken. Opvallend is de gevlochten dakconstructie die alle binnenruimten van het huis overspant. Omwille van het comfort is voor nagenoeg alle oppervlakten larikshout gebruikt.

El proyecto está destinado a una pareja con hijos que demandaba luz natural. La vivienda se compone de un dormitorio, un cuarto de los niños, un estudio, un comedor y una cocina. Destaca la estructura del techo en rejilla que abarca todos los habitáculos de la casa. En la mayoría de las superficies se ha utilizado la madera de alerce ya que proporciona confort al conjunto.

Il progetto è destinato a una coppia con figli che richiedeva luce naturale. L'abitazione è composta da una camera da letto, una camera per bambini, uno studio, sala da pranzo e cucina. Si distingue la struttura a rete del tetto, che comprende tutti gli abitacoli della casa. Il legno di larice è stato utilizzato per la maggior parte delle superfici, poiché apporta comfort all'insieme.

Este projeto foi concebido para um casal com filhos que pretendia luz natural. A casa compreende quarto de cama, quarto das crianças, escritório, sala de jantar e cozinha. Destaca-se a estrutura em grade do teto, que se estende a todas as divisões da casa. Na maior parte das superfícies foi utilizada a madeira de larício, que confere uma sensação de conforto ao conjunto.

Projektet är avsett för ett par med barn som ville ha dagsljus. Bostaden består av ett sovrum, barnens rum, arbetsrum, matsal och kök. Mest framträdande är en struktur av rutnät i taket som omfattar alla rum i huset. Lärkträ har använts på de flesta ytor, eftersom det bidrar med komfort till helheten.

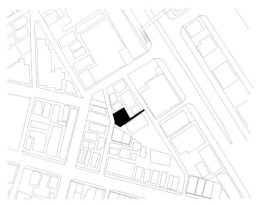

Site plan / Plan du site

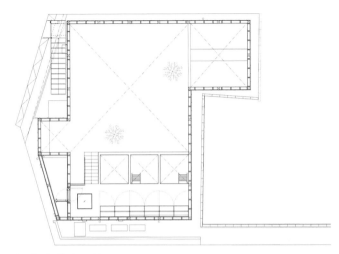

Second floor plan / Plan du second niveau

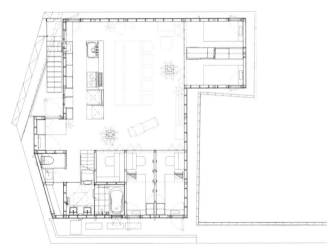

First floor plan / Plan du premier niveau

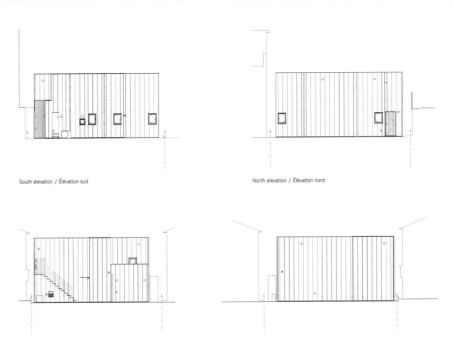

South elevation / Élévation sud

North elevation / Élévation nord

East elevation / Élévation est

West elevation / Élévation ouest

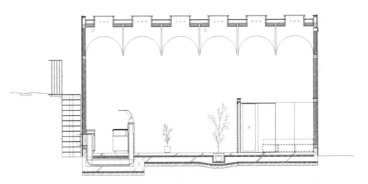

Section A / Coupe A

NEW RESIDENTIAL HOUSE
IN KYOTO TOWN

KYOTO, JAPAN
ALPHAVILLE – KENTARO TAKEGUCHI + ASAKO YAMAMOTO
www.a-ville.net | © Kei Sugino , Kentaro Takeguchi

This residential house is a response to the traditional wooden houses typical of the area. The most outstanding feature is the polyhedral shape of the walls, based on logical concepts and the performance of multiple functions. These walls blur the line between architecture and furniture design in order to stimulate perception.

Cette maison résidentielle répond à la structure traditionnelle des maisons en bois propres à la région. La principale caractéristique réside dans la forme polyédrique des cloisons, basée sur des concepts logiques et sur la réalisation des multiples fonctions. Les cloisons estompent les limites entre l'architecture et le mobilier pour stimuler la perception.

Dieses Wohnhaus nimmt die traditionelle Struktur der Holzhäuser wieder auf, die typisch für diese Gegend sind. Das wichtigste Merkmal ist die vielflächige Form der Trennwände, die auf logischen Entwürfen basieren und für viele Verwendungszwecke eingesetzt werden können. Die Trennwände kennzeichnen die Grenze zwischen der Architektur und den Möbeln, um die Wahrnehmung zu stimulieren.

Dit woonhuis is gebouwd volgens de traditionele constructie van de houten huizen die kenmerkend zijn voor deze regio. Het meest opvallend aan deze constructie zijn de veelvlakkige vormen van de scheidingswanden, waarbij is uitgegaan van logische concepten en het realiseren van meerdere functies. De scheidingswanden zorgen ervoor dat de grens tussen de bouwkunst en het meubilair vervaagt, zodat de waarneming wordt gestimuleerd.

Esta casa residencial responde a la estructura tradicional de casas de madera propias de la zona. El rasgo más característico es la forma poliédrica de los tabiques basada en conceptos lógicos y en la realización de múltiples funciones. Los tabiques desdibujan la frontera entre la arquitectura y el mobiliario para estimular la percepción.

Questa casa residenziale risponde alla struttura tradizionale delle case di legno tipiche della zona. Il tratto più caratteristico è la forma poliedrica dei tramezzi, che si basa su concetti logici e sulla realizzazione di molteplici funzioni. I tramezzi rendono indefinito il limite fra l'architettura e l'arredamento con il fine di stimolare la percezione.

Esta residência corresponde à estrutura tradicional das casas de madeira comuns na zona. O seu traço mais característico é a forma poliédrica das divisórias, baseada em conceitos lógicos e de multifuncionalidade. Estas divisórias desconstroem a fronteira entre a arquitetura e o mobiliário, com o objetivo de estimular a percepção.

Detta hem överensstämmer med den traditionella strukturen för trähus som är typisk för området. Det mest karakteristiska draget är den polyedriska formen för mellanväggarna, baserat på logiska egenskaper och på att uppfylla flera funktioner. Väggarna suddar ut gränsen mellan arkitektur och möbler för att stimulera upplevelsen.

Site plan / Plan du site

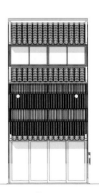

North elevation / Élévation nord

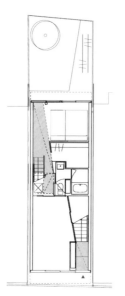

First floor plan / Plan du premier niveau

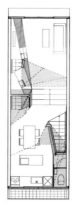

Second floor plan / Plan du deuxième niveau

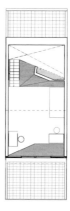

Third floor plan / Plan du troisième niveau

Conceptual scheme / Schémas conceptuels

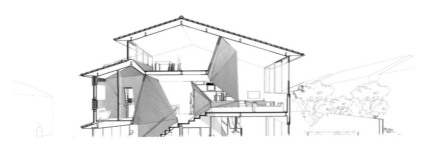

Sectional perspective / Coupe perspective

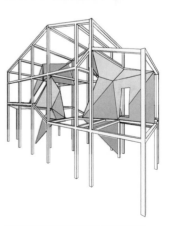

Frame and panel drawing / Dessin du châssis et des panneaux

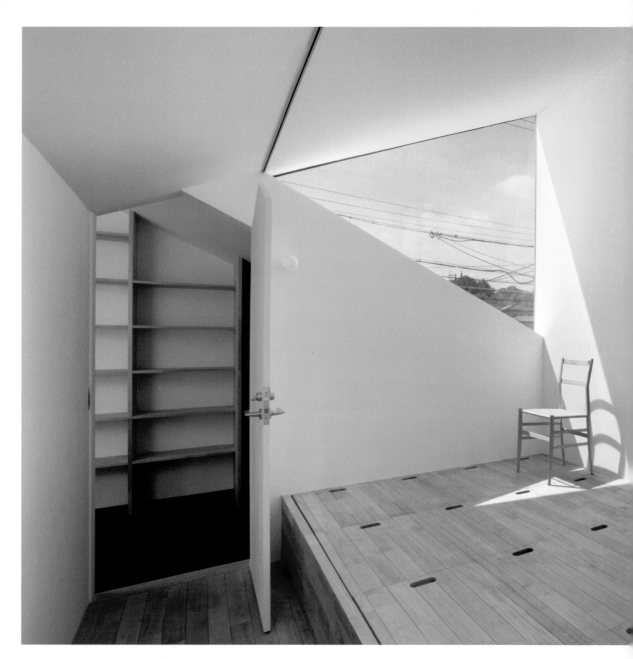

COMPLEX RESIDENTIAL HOUSE
IN NAGOYA

NAGOYA, JAPAN
TOMOHIRO HATA ARCHITECT & ASSOCIATES
www.hata-archi.com | © Noriyuki Yano

The house was planned as if it were a small wood-lined room. Inside, every space hides openings that serve as entrances, lifts, windows and viewing balconies. A minimalist contrast was sought and generously provided by the whiteness of the walls against the earthy look of the wooden flooring.

Le logement est conçu comme une petite habitation recouverte de bois. À l'intérieur, chaque espace dissimule des ouvertures qui font office d'accès, d'élévations, de fenêtres et de balcons fermés. Le contraste minimaliste du blanc des murs avec le dessin terreux propre au bois dans le sol a été recherché volontairement.

Das Haus wurde so geplant, als wenn es sich um ein kleines, mit Holz ausgekleidetes Zimmer handeln würde. In seinem Inneren verbergen sich in jedem Raum Öffnungen, die als Zugänge, Erhebungen, Fenster und Balkone oder Erker dienen. Man hat sich bewusst für den minimalistischen Kontrast zwischen den weißen Wänden und der erdigen Zeichnung des Holzes im Fußboden entschieden.

Het ontwerp is ontstaan vanuit de gedachte van een kleine met hout beklede kamer. In het interieur zijn in elke ruimte verborgen openingen die dienen als toegang, verhoging, raam of uitkijkpunt. Er is bewust gezocht naar een minimalistisch contrast tussen het wit van de muren en de okerkleurige tekening in de houten vloer.

La vivienda ha sido planificada como si de una pequeña habitación forrada de madera se tratara. Dentro de ella cada espacio esconde aperturas que funcionan como accesos, elevaciones, ventanas y balcones miradores. Se ha buscado de manera voluntaria el contraste minimalista del blanco de las paredes con el dibujo terroso propio de la madera en el suelo.

L'abitazione fu progettata come se si trattasse di una piccola stanza foderata di legno. Al suo interno, ogni spazio nasconde aperture che fungono da accessi, rialzamenti, finestre e verande. È stato ricercato intenzionalmente il contrasto minimalista tra il bianco delle pareti e il disegno terroso caratteristico del legno sul pavimento.

Esta casa foi projetada como se se tratasse de uma pequena sala forrada de madeira. No interior, cada espaço esconde aberturas que funcionam como acessos, elevações, janelas e varandas. Procurou-se propositadamente o contraste minimalista do branco das paredes com a cor terrosa da madeira no chão.

Bostaden planerades som om det vore ett litet träfodrat rum det handlade om. Varje utrymme på insidan döljer öppningar som fungerar som ingångar, förhöjningar, fönster och balkonger. Man har medvetet sökt den minimalistiska kontrasten mellan det vita på väggarna och trägolvets naturliga mönster.

Roof plan / plan du toit

Second floor plan / Plan du second niveau

First floor plan / Plan du premier niveau

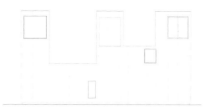

East elevation / Élévation est

West elevation / Élévation ouest

South elevation / Élévation sud

North elevation / Élévation nord

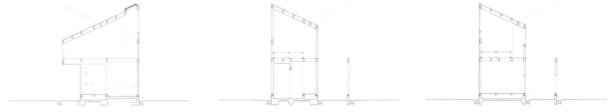

Sections / Coupes

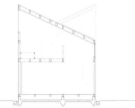

Sections / Coupes

HOUSE IN
HIKARIMACHI II

KASUGA, JAPAN
KENICHIRO IDE / RHYTHMDESIGN
www.rhythmdesign.org | © Koichi Torimura

This residential dwelling was constructed using reinforced concrete and a large wooden structure. As is customary in Japan, urban land for building determines the size of the house: 13 m wide and 5 m long. Wood was chosen as the material for the structure because of its suitability for the high humidity of the Japanese climate.

Ce logement résidentiel a été construit avec du béton armé et une grande structure en bois. Comme de coutume au Japon, le terrain urbain de la construction a déterminé la création de la maison sur 13 m de long et 5 m de large. La structure en bois a été choisie car ce matériau est celui qui s'adapte le mieux à la forte humidité du climat japonais.

Dieses Wohnhaus wurde aus Stahlbeton und einer großen Holzstruktur errichtet. Wie es in Japan üblich ist, wurde der Bau des Hauses von dem städtischen Gelände auf eine Breite von 13 m und eine Länge von 5 m festgelegt. Man entschied sich für eine Holzstruktur, da es das Material ist, das sich am besten an das feuchte japanische Klima anpasst.

Dit woongebouw is opgetrokken uit gewapend beton en heeft een groot houten skelet. Voor het bouwen van een huis binnen stedelijk gebied in Japan is er normaliter een oppervlakte beschikbaar van 13 m breedte en 5 m lengte. Er is gekozen voor een houten constructie omdat hout zich het best aanpast aan de hoge vochtigheid van het Japanse klimaat.

Esta vivienda residencial se construyó empleando hormigón armado y una gran estructura de madera-. Como es habitual en Japón, el terreno urbano para la construcción determinó la creación de la casa de 13 m de ancho y 5 m de largo. Se eligió la estructura de madera porque es el material que mejor se adapta a la elevada humedad del clima japonés.

Questa casa residenziale fu edificata utilizzando cemento armato e una grande struttura di legno. Come d'abitudine in Giappone, il terreno urbano per la costruzione ha determinato la costruzione della casa di 13 m di larghezza e 5 m di altezza. Fu scelta la struttura di legno in quanto materiale che meglio si adatta all'alto livello di umidità del clima giapponese.

Esta moradia foi construída com betão armado e uma grande estrutura de madeira. Como é habitual no Japão, o terreno disponível para construção limitou as dimensões da casa a 5 m de largura por 13 m de comprimento. Optou-se por uma estrutura em madeira por ser este o material que melhor se adapta à elevada umidade do clima japonês.

Denna villa uppfördes med hjälp av armerad betong och en stor stomme av trä. Som brukligt vid konstruktion av stadsbebyggelse i Japan bestämdes måtten för husbygget, som är 13 m brett och 5 m långt, efter marktillgången. Man valde att använda sig av en stomme av trä eftersom detta material är bäst anpassat till det japanska klimatets höga luftfuktighet.

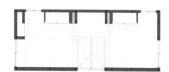

Third floor plan / Plan du troisième niveau

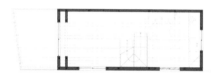

Second floor plan / Plan du deuxième niveau

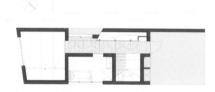

First floor plan / Plan du premier niveau

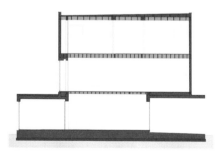

Section / Coupe

TWO-STOREY
RESIDENTIAL HOUSES
IN LIZUKA

IIZUKA, JAPAN
KENICHIRO IDE / RHYTHMDESIGN
www.rhythmdesign.org | © Koichi Torimura

This is a wooden two-storey apartment complex located in a village on the outskirts of Lizuka, in southern Japan. The special nature of the land led to the house being built in a triangular, umbrella-like shape. The dining room is outstanding; it is situated in the centre of the house, from where you can see the other rooms.

Ce projet appartient à un complexe d'appartements de deux étages avec structure en bois, situé dans un village proche de Lizuka, au sud du Japon. La particularité du terrain a impliqué la construction en forme triangulaire semblable à un parapluie. La salle à manger, d'où l'on peut voir les autres pièces, se trouve au milieu de la maison.

Der Apartmentkomplex aus zwei Wohnungen mit einer Holzstruktur befindet sich in einem Dorf in der Nähe von Lizuka, im Süden Japans. Die Einzigartigkeit des Geländes sorgte dafür, dass das Haus dreieckig konstruiert wurde, ähnlich wie ein Schirm. Ins Auge fällt das Esszimmer, welches sich im Mittelpunkt des Hauses befindet und von dem aus man in die anderen Zimmer sehen kann.

Dit appartementencomplex van twee verdiepingen heeft een houten constructie. Het staat in een dorp in de omgeving van Lizuka, in het zuiden van Japan. Door de specifieke eigenschappen van het terrein is de woning in een driehoekige vorm gebouwd, als een paraplu. Opvallend is dat de eethoek zich midden in het huis bevindt. Van daaruit is er zicht op alle andere kamers.

Complejo de apartamentos de dos pisos con estructura de madera situado en un pueblo a las afueras de Lizuka, en la parte sur de Japón. La singularidad del terreno hizo que la vivienda se construyera en forma triangular, semejante a un paraguas. Destaca el comedor situado en el centro de la casa desde donde se puede ver el resto de habitaciones.

Complesso di appartamenti di due piani con struttura in legno situato in un paese nella periferia di Lizuka, al sud del Giappone. La particolarità del terreno ha fatto sì che l'abitazione si costruisse a forma triangolare, simile ad un ombrello. Si distingue la sala da pranzo situata al centro della casa, da cui è possibile vedere le altre stanze.

Complexo de apartamentos de dois pisos com estrutura em madeira, situado numa aldeia dos arredores de Lizuka, no sul do Japão. As peculiaridades do terreno levaram à construção de um edifício com uma forma triangular, semelhante à de um chapéu de chuva. Destaca-se a zona de refeições no centro, da casa, de onde se podem ver todas as outras divisões.

Lägenhetskomplex med två våningar i träkonstruktion är beläget i en by i utkanten av Lizuka, i södra Japan. Den unika tomten gjorde att huset byggdes i en trekantig form, liknandes ett paraply. Mest framträdande är matsalen i mitten av huset, varifrån man kan se resten av bostaden.

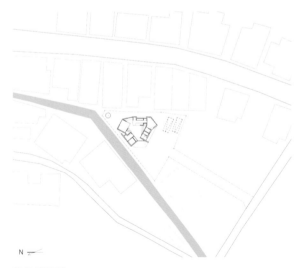

N

Site plan / Plan du site

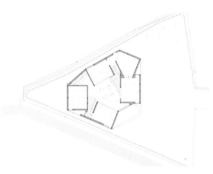

Second floor plan / Plan du second niveau

First floor plan / Plan du premier niveau

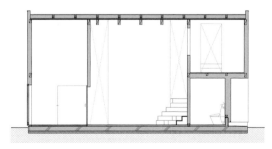

Section / Coupe

WOODEN STRUCTURE
BELLY HOUSE

KYOTO, JAPAN
TOMOHIRO HATA ARCHITECT & ASSOCIATES
www.hata-archi.com | © Noriyuki Yano

The project was conceived as a large tree whose core consists of a large wooden frame leaning on its exterior. The structure is perforated with openings that serve as windows, doors and entrances. Thanks to this original and unique structure, the space around this core can be arranged freely.

Le projet a été conçu comme un grand arbre dont le cœur est constitué d'une structure en bois qui s'appuie sur l'extérieur. La structure est percée par des ouvertures qui font office de fenêtres, de portes et d'accès. Grâce à cet agencement original et particulier, l'espace peut être organisé librement autour de ce cœur.

Das Projekt wurde wie ein großer Baum konzipiert, dessen Kern durch eine große Holzstruktur gebildet wird, die sich auf den äußeren Bereich stützt. Die Struktur ist von Öffnungen durchzogen, die als Fenster, Türen und Zugänge genutzt werden. Bedingt durch diese ungewöhnliche und besondere Struktur, kann der Raum frei um diesen Kern herum gestaltet werden.

Dit ontwerp gaat uit van een grote boom waarvan de kern wordt gevormd door een grote houten constructie die van buitenaf wordt ondersteund. In de constructie zijn openingen gemaakt die dienen als ramen, deuren en ingangen. Door de originele en bijzondere structuur kan de ruimte rondom de kern vrij worden ingevuld.

El proyecto es concebido como un gran árbol cuyo núcleo está formado por una gran estructura de madera que se apoya en el exterior. La estructura está agujereada con aberturas que funcionan como ventanas, puertas y accesos. Debido a esta original y particular estructura, el espacio se puede organizar libremente en torno a este núcleo.

Il progetto fu concepito come un grande albero il cui nucleo è costituito da una grande struttura di legno appoggiata sull'esterno. La struttura è bucherellata con aperture che funzionano come finestre, porte e accessi. Grazie a questa originale e peculiare struttura, è possibile organizzare liberamente lo spazio attorno al nucleo.

O projeto foi concebido como uma árvore enorme, cujo núcleo é constituído por uma grande estrutura em madeira apoiada no exterior. A referida estrutura apresenta-se perfurada por aberturas que funcionam como janelas, portas e acessos. Graças a esta estrutura especial tão original, o espaço pode ser organizado livremente em torno do núcleo central.

Man tänkte sig projektet som ett stort träd vavrs kärna utgörs av en stor trästruktur som vilar på det yttre. Strukturen är perforerad med öppningar som fungerar som fönster, dörrar och ingångar. På grund av denna originella och speciella struktur kan utrymmet kring denna kärna arrangeras fritt.

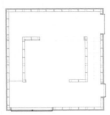

Thrid floor plan / Plan du troisième étage

Second floor plan / Plan du deuxième étage

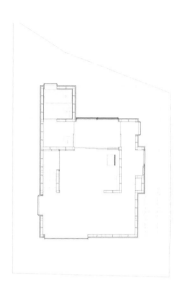

First floor plan / Plan du premier étage

Basement plan / Plan du sous-sol

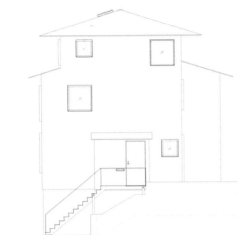

Elevations / Élévations

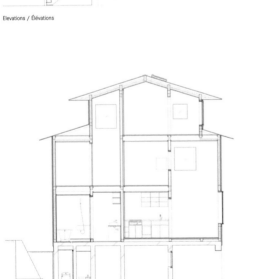

Sections / Coupes

HOUSE FOR
HEARING HANDICAPPED
PERSONS ROOM ROOM

TOKYO, JAPAN
TAKESHI HOSAKA ARCHITECTS
www.hosakatakeshi.com | © Koji Fujii

The owners of this house have a hearing impairment, which determined the design: a box with many small openings of 200 mm² used as communication points between the two floors and as provision for natural light to enter to aid vision. Wood is used for the flooring and furniture to provide comfort.

Les propriétaires de cette habitation présentent un handicap auditif qui a conditionné la conception du lieu: une boîte avec de nombreuses petites ouvertures de 200 mm² utilisées comme espaces de communication entre les deux étages et arrivée de lumière naturelle pour assurer une bonne visibilité. Le bois est utilisé pour les sols et le mobilier en raison de son aspect confortable.

Die Eigentümer dieses Wohnhauses haben eine Hörbehinderung, was Einfluss auf das Design hatte: eine Kiste mit vielen kleinen Öffnungen von 200 mm², die als Atrien und Kommunikationsorte zwischen den Stockwerken dienen und für den natürlichen Lichteinfall sorgen, um dadurch die Sicht zu verbessern. Holz wurde bei den Böden und den Möbeln verwendet, um Behaglichkeit zu vermitteln.

De eigenaren van deze woning hebben een gehoorstoornis die bepalend is geweest voor het ontwerp: een vierkant met heel veel kleine openingen van 200 mm² die zijn gebruikt als communicatieruimten tussen de twee verdiepingen en om de natuurlijke lichtinval voor het zicht te ondersteunen. Omwille van het comfort is hout gebruikt voor de vloeren en het meubilair.

Los propietarios de esta vivienda tienen una minusvalía en la audición que condicionó el diseño: una caja con muchas aberturas pequeñas de 200 mm² utilizadas como espacios de comunicación entre los dos pisos y como entrada de luz natural para ayudar en la visión. La madera es utilizada en suelos y mobiliario para proporcionar confort.

I proprietari di quest'edificio presentano una disabilità uditiva che ne ha condizionato il design: una scatola con molte piccole aperture di 200 mm² utilizzate come spazi di comunicazione tra i due piani e come punti di ingresso di luce naturale per agevolare la vista. Il legno è utilizzato nei pavimenti e arredamento per offrire comfort.

Os proprietários desta casa são portadores de deficiência auditiva, o que condicionou o projeto: uma caixa com muitas aberturas pequenas de 200 mm² utilizadas como espaços de comunicação entre os dois andares e para a entrada de luz natural, de modo a melhorar a visibilidade. A madeira foi utilizada nos pavimentos e mobiliário para proporcionar mais conforto.

Ägarna av denna bostad är hörselskadade vilket påverkat designen: en låda med många små öppningar på 200 mm² som används, utrymmen för förbindelse mellan de två våningarna och öppning för dagsljus för att göra det lättare att se. Man använder trä i golv och möbler för komfort.

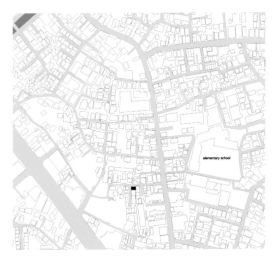

Site plan / Plan du site

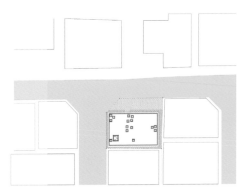

Site plan / Plan du site

Roof plan / Plan du toit

Elevation / Élévation

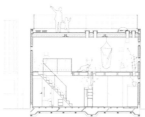

Sections / Coupes

Second floor plan / Plan du second niveau

First floor plan / Plan du premier niveau

OUTSIDE IN
YAMANASHI HOUSE

TOKYO, JAPAN
TAKESHI HOSAKA ARCHITECTS
www.hosakatakeshi.com | © Koji Fujii

The remodelling of a house allowed the owners to establish a close harmony with the natural surroundings of the house. To achieve this, they chose wood as the main material for the interior design. The furniture, doors, windows and floor were created with different types of treated wood that create different shades and patterns.

La transformation d'une habitation a permis aux propriétaires d'obtenir une harmonie avec la nature proche. C'est dans cette optique qu'ils ont choisi le bois pour la conception intérieure. Le mobilier, les portes, les fenêtres et le sol ont été construits avec différents types de bois traité qui créent plusieurs tonalités et motifs.

Die Umgestaltung eines Wohnhauses ermöglichte dem Eigentümer eine wirkliche Einheit mit der Natur, von der das Wohnhaus umgeben ist. In diesem Sinne wählten Sie Holz als vorherrschendes Material für das Innenraumdesign aus. Die Möbel, Türen, Fenster und der Boden wurden aus unterschiedlich behandelten Holzarten gebaut, die verschiedene Farbtöne und Zeichnungen haben.

Met de verbouwing van hun woning hebben de eigenaren een perfecte harmonie met de omliggende omgeving weten te bewerkstelligen. Voor het ontwerp van het interieur hebben ze gekozen voor hout als belangrijkste materiaal. Het meubilair, de deuren, de ramen en de vloer zijn gemaakt van verschillende behandelde houtsoorten waardoor verschillende kleurschakeringen en patronen zijn ontstaan.

La remodelación de una vivienda permitió que los propietarios armonizaran con la naturaleza situada cerca de la casa. En este sentido eligieron la madera como material protagonista del diseño interior. El mobiliario, las puertas, las ventanas y el suelo fueron construidos con distintos tipos de madera tratada que crean diferentes tonalidades y dibujos.

La ristrutturazione di un edificio ha permesso ai proprietari di stabilire la giusta armonia con la natura ad esso vicina. In questo senso hanno scelto il legno come materiale protagonista del design degli interni. L'arredamento, le porte, le finestre ed il pavimento sono stati costruiti con diversi tipi di legni trattati che danno vita a tonalità e disegni differenti.

A remodelação de uma vivenda permitiu aos proprietários estabelecer uma correta harmonia com a natureza envolvente. Neste sentido, a madeira foi escolhida como material protagonista no design interior. O mobiliário, portas, janelas e pavimento foram executados com diferentes tipos de madeiras tratadas, gerando diferentes tonalidades e desenhos.

Ombyggnaden av ett hem gjorde det möjligt för ägarna att upprätta rätt harmoni med naturen som omger bostaden. De valde därför trä som det viktigaste materialet i interiördesignen. Möbler, dörrar, fönster och golvet byggdes med olika typer av behandlat virke som skapar olika nyanser och mönster.

Site plan / Plan du site

Section detail / Coupe de détail

Section / Coupe

BOXES OF
THE TEX-TONIC HOUSE 1

LONDON, UNITED KINGDOM
PAUL McANEARY ARCHITECTS
www.paulmcaneary.com | © Paul McAneary Architects

The client's desire was to create a spacious, high volume loft uniting the contemporary and the functional. The architects' response to their request was close attention to detail, even developing a new material: cast bronze timber. The elements revolve around the wood to highlight its beautiful texture.

Le client souhaitait créer un loft spacieux et volumineux qui allie modernité et fonctionnalité. Les architectes ont répondu à sa demande en accordant une attention particulière aux détails, en développant notamment un nouveau matériau : le bois en bronze fondu. Les éléments tournent autour du bois pour souligner sa jolie texture.

Der Wunsch des Kunden war die Erschaffung eines geräumigen Lofts mit viel Platz, das Modernität und Funktionalität in sich vereint. Die Antwort der Architekten auf diese Vorgabe war die besondere Aufmerksamkeit für Details und sogar die Entwicklung eines neuen Materials: in Bronze gegossenes Holz. Die Elemente drehen sich um das Holz, um seine wunderschöne Textur herauszuheben.

De opdrachtgever vroeg een ruime, grote loft te ontwerpen waarin eigentijdsheid en functionaliteit met elkaar samen zouden gaan. Daarop antwoordden de architecten met zeer precieze aandacht voor details en bovendien ontwikkelden ze een nieuw materiaal: in hout gegoten brons. Daarnaast zijn allerlei elementen gebruikt die de prachtige textuur van het hout onderstrepen.

El cliente deseaba la creación de unos espacios abiertos de gran volumen que aunara contemporaneidad y funcionalidad. La respuesta de los arquitectos a este requisito fue la atención precisa a los detalles, e incluso se desarrolló un nuevo material: la madera de bronce fundido. Los elementos giran en torno a la madera para resaltar su hermosa textura.

Il desiderio del cliente era la creazione di un loft spazioso di grande volume che unisse contemporaneità e funzionalità. La risposta degli architetti alla sua richiesta è stata l'attenzione precisa ai dettagli, anche con lo sviluppo di un nuovo materiale: il legno bronzato. Gli elementi ruotano attorno al legno per esaltare la sua piacevole venatura.

O cliente pretendia um loft espaço, de grande volumetria, que conjugasse contemporaneidade e funcionalidade. A resposta dos arquitetos foi uma atenção minuciosa aos pormenores, desenvolvendo inclusivamente um material completamente novo: a madeira de bronze fundido. Todos os elementos giram em torno da madeira, fazendo sobressair a beleza da sua textura.

Kundens begäran var skapandet av en stor, rymlig och öppen yta som förenade modernitet och funktionalitet. Arkitekternas svar på önskemålet var uppmärksamhet på detaljer, man utvecklade till och med ett nytt material: trä av smält brons. Elementen kretsar kring träet för att belysa dess vackra textur.

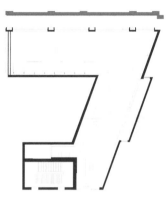

Mezzanine floor plan / plan de la mezzanine

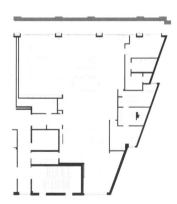

Ground floor plan / Plan du rez-de-chaussée

BROOKLINE HOUSE
IN A SUBURB OF BOSTON

BROOKLINE, MA, USA
JONATHAN LEVI ARCHITECTS
www.leviarc.com | © Nick Wheeler Photographics, Jonathan Levi Architects

The colour and height of this six-story house create a resemblance to the trees that surround it. This vertical dynamic is expressed in the interior via independent spaces which require ingenious solutions. The choice of wood as the main material for the interior and exterior meets the criteria for integration with nature.

Cette habitation de six étages se distingue par sa couleur et sa hauteur, semblables aux arbres qui l'entourent. Ce développement vertical s'exprime à l'intérieur par le biais d'espaces indépendants qui requièrent des solutions ingénieuses. Le choix du bois à l'intérieur et à l'extérieur répond au critère d'intégration dans la nature.

Das Wohnhaus mit sechs Stockwerken fällt auf durch seine Farbgebung und die Höhe. Es ist fast so hoch wie die Bäume, die es umgeben. Diese vertikale Entwicklung wird im Innenraum durch unabhängige Räume ausgedrückt, die erfinderische Lösungen benötigten. Durch die Auswahl von Holz als Hauptbaumaterial für sowohl den Innen- als auch den Außenraum wird dem Kriterium Rechnung getragen, sich in die Natur zu integrieren.

Dit gebouw van zes verdiepingen valt op door zijn kleuren en hoogte, die overeenstemmen met de bomen rondom het huis. Deze verticale groeirichting komt ook tot uiting in het interieur. De onafhankelijke ruimten vragen om ingenieuze oplossingen. Er is gekozen voor hout als belangrijkste materiaal voor het interieur en het exterieur, om te kunnen voldoen aan de voorwaarde dat het huis zou worden ingepast in de omliggende natuur.

La vivienda de seis plantas destaca por su colorido y su altura, semejantes a los árboles que la rodean. Este desarrollo vertical se expresa en el interior a través de espacios independientes que requieren soluciones ingeniosas. La elección de la madera como material protagonista del interior y del exterior sigue el criterio de integración con la naturaleza.

L'edificio di sei piani colpisce per il colorito e per l'altezza, tratti simili a quelli degli alberi che la circondano. Questo sviluppo verticale si esprime all'interno attraverso spazi indipendenti che richiedono soluzioni ingegnose. La scelta del legno come materiale protagonista dell'interno e dell'esterno segue il criterio di integrazione nella natura.

A casa de seis andares destaca-se pelas suas cores e altura, semelhantes às das árvores que a rodeiam. Este desenvolvimento vertical traduz-se no interior por uma série de espaços interdependentes, que requerem soluções engenhosas. A escolha da madeira como material protagonista tanto do interior como do exterior obedece ao critério de integração na natureza.

Sexvåningshuset utmärker sig för färgen och höjden, och det efterliknar de träd som omger det. Denna vertikala utveckling uttrycks på insidan genom separata utrymmen som kräver sinnrika lösningar. Valet av trä som det viktigaste materialet på in- och utsidan följer kriterierna om att integrera med naturen.

Second basement level / Deuxième sous-sol

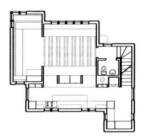

First basement level / Premier sous-sol

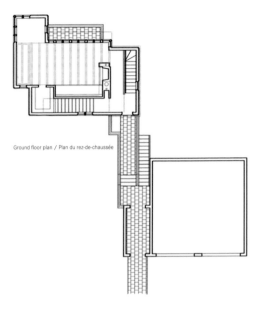

Ground floor plan / Plan du rez-de-chaussée

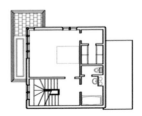

Second floor plan / Plan du deuxième niveau

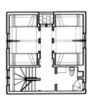

Third floor plan / Plan du troisième niveau

Fourth floor plan / Plan du quatrième niveau

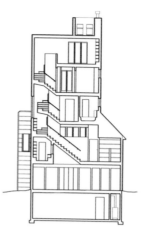

Sections / Coupes

REMODELED
HISTORIC HOUSE
IN LA CORUÑA

LA CORUÑA, SPAIN
MIYARD
www.miyarq.com | © Miyard

This project is a reconstruction of a 40 m² house located in the historic centre of this Galician city. Given the small size of the site, optimization of space is a focus throughout the project. Used extensively in the carpentry, furniture and floors, the wood really stands out from the other materials used.

Ce projet est la transformation d'une habitation de 40 m² située dans le centre historique de la ville galicienne. Étant donné les petites dimensions du terrain, les espaces sont optimisés dans l'ensemble du projet. Parmi les matériaux utilisés, on distingue le bois, utilisé massivement dans la menuiserie, le mobilier et les sols.

Dieses Projekt ist die Neuerrichtung eines Wohnhauses auf 40 m², das sich im historischen Teil der galizischen Stadt befindet. Aufgrund der geringen Fläche des Bauplatzes, wurden im gesamten Projekt die Räume optimiert. Bei den verwendeten Materialien fällt das Holz besonders auf, das verschwenderisch bei den Holzelementen, den Möbeln und den Böden verwendet wurde.

Dit gebouw is ontstaan met de herbouw van een woning van 40 m² in het historische centrum van La Coruña, een stad in het Spaanse Galicië. Gezien de beperkte afmetingen van het perceel zijn alle ruimten binnen het gebouw optimaal benut. Van alle toegepaste materialen valt het gebruikte hout het meest op. Het is op grote schaal gebruikt voor het timmerwerk, het meubilair en de vloeren.

Este proyecto es una reedificación de una vivienda de 40 m² situada en el centro histórico de la ciudad gallega. Dadas las reducidas dimensiones del solar, la optimización de espacios está presente en todo el proyecto. De entre los materiales utilizados, destaca la madera utilizada masivamente en la carpintería, el mobiliario y el suelo.

Questo progetto è un rifacimento di un edificio di 40 m² situato nel centro storico della città gallega. Considerate le dimensioni ridotte dell'area, l'ottimizzazione degli spazi permea tutto il progetto. Tra i vari materiali utilizzati si distingue il legno, impiegato considerevolmente in serramenti, arredamento e pavimenti.

Este projeto consistiu na reedificação de uma casa de 40 m² situada no centro histórico da cidade galega. Dadas as reduzidas dimensões do terreno, a otimização de espaços domina todo o projeto. Entre os materiais utilizados destaca-se a madeira, utilizada massivamente na carpintaria, mobiliário e pavimentos.

Detta projekt är en rekonstruktion av en bostad på 40 m², belägen i den galiciska stadens historiska centrum. Med tanke på att tomten är väldigt liten har man genom hela projektet försökt att utnyttja utrymmet optimalt. Bland de material som används är trä det mest framträdande, framför allt i snickeri, möbler och golv.

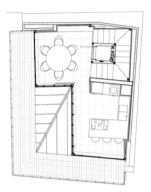

Fourth floor plan / Plan du quatrième niveau

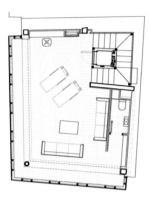

Thrid floor plan / Plan du troisième niveau

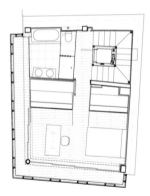

Second floor plan / Plan du deuxième niveau

First floor plan / Plan du premier niveau

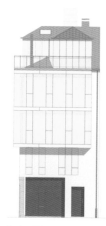

Elevations / Élévations

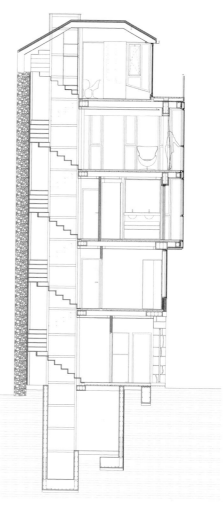

Section / Coupe

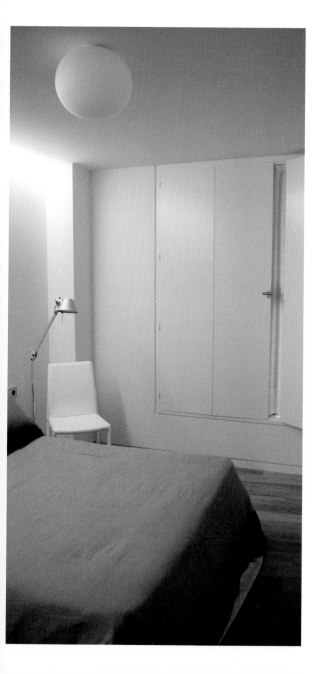

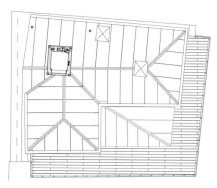

Roof plan / Plan du toit

ALBRECHT RESIDENCE
WITH VIEWS OVER
THE MISSISSIPPI RIVER

RED WING, MO, USA
SALMELA ARCHITECT
www.salmelaarchitect.com | © Peter Bastianelli Kerze

Five different types of wood, including reused spruce and cypress beams from old buildings, were used in the construction of the house. One of the features that really stands out, guiding the way into the house, is a covered pergola located on one side. This also marks the transition, via a garden, between the street and interior.

Pour construire cette habitation, cinq types de bois ont été utilisés, ainsi que des poutres anciennes en sapin et en cyprès d'anciens bâtiments. Parmi tous les espaces, on distingue une pergola couverte, située sur l'un des côtés, qui indique l'accès et marque la transition, par le biais d'un jardin, entre la rue et l'intérieur.

Beim Bau des Wohnhauses wurden fünf verschiedene Holzarten verwendet und man nutzte Balken aus Tanne und Zypresse aus alten Gebäuden. Zwischen all den Räumen sticht eine überdachte Pergola an einer der Seiten hervor. Sie fungiert als Richtungsweiser zum Eingang des Hauses und markiert den Übergang von der Straße zum Innenraum, der durch einen Garten führt.

Voor de bouw van dit huis zijn vijf verschillende soorten hout gebruikt en zijn oude sparren- en cipressenhouten balken uit oude gebouwen hergebruikt. Van alle ruimten valt vooral het overdekte prieeltje op dat aan een van de vleugels is gebouwd. Het fungeert als toegangswijzer naar het huis en markeert – via een tuin – de overgang tussen de straat en het interieur.

En la construcción de la vivienda se utilizaron cinco tipos de madera y se aprovecharon vigas antiguas de abeto y ciprés de viejos edificios. De todos los espacios destaca una pérgola cubierta situada en uno de los lados que funciona como indicador del acceso a la casa y marca la transición, a través de un jardín, entre la calle y el interior.

Durante la costruzione dell'abitazione sono stati utilizzati cinque tipi diversi di legno e sono state sfruttate vecchie travi di abete e cipresso di antichi edifici. Tra i vari spazi si distingue una pergola coperta situata in una delle parti laterali che funziona come indicazione di accesso alla casa e segna il passaggio, attraverso il giardino, tra la strada e l'interno.

Na construção desta residência foram usados cinco tipos de madeira diferentes e reaproveitaram-se vigas antigas de abeto e cipreste provenientes de outros edifícios. Entre todos os espaços destaca-se uma pérgula coberta, situada numa das laterais, que funciona como indicador do acesso à casa e marca, através de um jardim, a transição entre o exterior e o interior.

I byggandet av bostaden användes fem olika träslag och man tog till vara på bjälkar av gran och cypress från gamla byggnader. Bland alla utrymmen utmärker sig en pergola belägen på den sidan som fungerar som en fingervisning om ingången till huset och markerar övergången, genom en trädgård, mellan gatan och insidan.

Second floor plan / Plan du second niveau

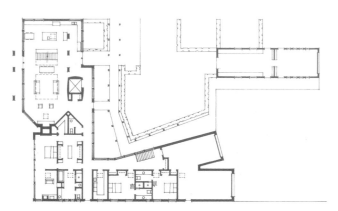

Ground floor plan / Plan du rez-de-chaussée

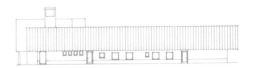

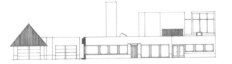

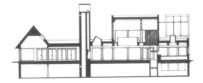

Sections and elevations / Coupes et élévations

Sections and elevations / Coupes et élévations

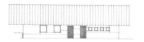

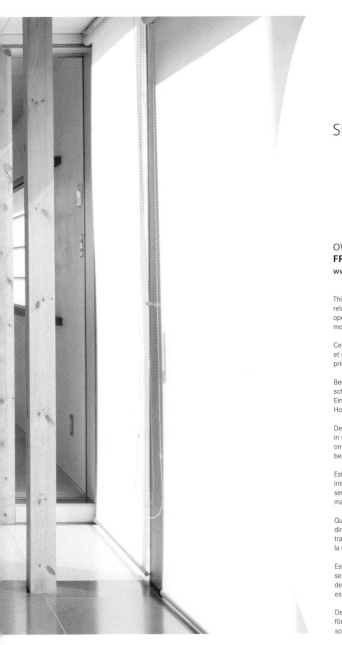

SPACE LAYERING OF
N-HOUSE

OWANI, JAPAN
FRANK LA RIVIÈRE ARCHITECTS, INC.
www.frank-la-riviere.com | © Frank la Rivière Architects, Inc.

This residence was built on a low budget with the idea of creating spaces that stand in direct relationship to each other by means of transition zones in order to create a general feeling of openness and transparency. The birch plywood and wooden column principal structure are the most outstanding elements of the project.

Cette résidence à petit budget est conçue pour privilégier une impression générale d'ouverture et de transparence. Le contreplacage en bouleau et la colonne en bois en tant que structure principale sont les éléments les plus caractéristiques du projet.

Bei diesem Wohnhaus, das mit einem geringen Budget gebaut werden musste, wollte man Räume schaffen, die durch Übergangsbereiche in direktem Verhältnis zueinander stehen, um so den Eindruck von allgemeiner Offenheit und Transparenz zu kreieren. Das Birkenfurnierholz und die Holzsäule als wichtigste Struktur, sind die charakteristischsten Elemente dieses Projekts.

Deze lowbudgetwoning is gebouwd met de intentie om ruimten te creëren die direct met elkaar in verbinding staan via overgangsgebieden, zodat een algemeen gevoel van ruimte en openheid ontstaat. De meest kenmerkende elementen van dit ontwerp zijn het gebruik van gelaagd berkenhout en de houten pilaar die de belangrijkste constructie vormt.

Esta residencia de bajo presupuesto se construyó con la idea de generar espacios que se interpusieran en relación directa entre sí por medio de zonas de transición para crear una sensación de apertura y transparencia general. El contrachapado de abedul y la columna de madera como estructura principal son los elementos definitorios del proyecto.

Questa residenza a basso budget fu costruita con l'idea di dare vita a spazi che si frapponessero direttamente tra di loro tramite zone di transizione, per creare una sensazione di apertura e trasparenza generale. Gli elementi più caratteristici del progetto sono il compensato di betulla e la colonna di legno come struttura principale.

Esta residência de orçamento bastante baixo foi construída com a ideia de criar espaços que se relacionassem diretamente entre si através de zonas de transição, criando uma sensação de abertura e transparência gerais. O contraplacado de bétula e a coluna de madeira como estrutura principal são os elementos mais caraterísticos do projeto.

Denna lågbudgetvilla byggdes med idén om att skapa utrymmen som korsar varandra som zoner för övergång för att skapa en allmänt öppen och luftig känsla. Plywood av björk och pelare av trä som huvudstruktur är de mest karakteristiska delarna av projektet.

North elevation / Élévation nord

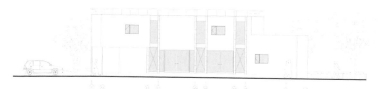

South elevation / Élévation sud

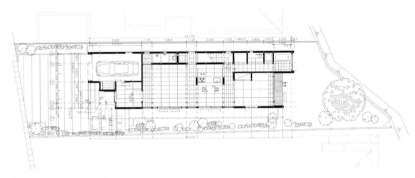

Second floor plan / Plan du second niveau

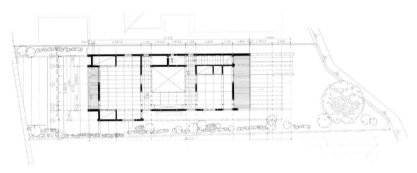

First floor plan / Plan du premier niveau

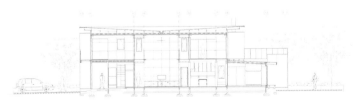

Section / Coupe

East elevation / Élévation est

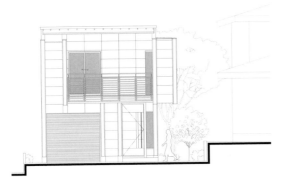

West elevation / Élévation ouest

THE IDYLLIC SETTING OF
THE AIR HOUSE

HAGI, JAPAN
SAMBUICHI ARCHITECTS
samb@d2.dion.ne.jp | © Hiroyuki Hirai

Situated on the island of Honshu, near Shizuki castle and the Hashimoto River, this house was designed with horizontal frames. Wooden panels arranged lengthwise reinforce the sensation of fluidity and provide natural ventilation. Ceilings and floors are finished with wood that provides soundproofing and absorbs moisture.

L'habitation, située près du château de Shizuki et du fleuve Hashimoto, sur l'île de Honshu, a été conçue avec des structures horizontales. Les panneaux de bois disposés dans la longueur renforcent l'impression de fluidité et permettent une ventilation naturelle. Les toits et les sols sont réalisés en bois pour son isolation acoustique et son absorption de l'humidité.

Das Wohnhaus, das sich in der Nähe des Schlosses Shizuki und des Flusses Hashimoto, auf der Insel Honshu befindet, wurde mit horizontalen Strukturen entworfen. Die längsgerichteten Holzpaneele verstärken den fließenden Eindruck und sorgen für eine natürliche Belüftung. Dach und Böden wurden aus Holz gefertigt, das schallisolierend wirkt und Feuchtigkeit absorbiert.

Deze woning bevindt zich in de buurt van het kasteel Shizuki en de rivier Hashimoto, op het Japanse eiland Honshu. Voor het ontwerp is gebruikgemaakt van horizontale constructies. Doordat de houten panelen in de lengte zijn verwerkt, wordt de vloeiende beweging versterkt en ontstaat natuurlijke ventilatie. Het hout waarmee de plafonds en vloeren zijn afgewerkt zorgt voor akoestische isolatie en absorbeert de vochtigheid.

La vivienda, situada cerca del castillo Shizuki y del río Hashimoto, en la isla de Honshu, fue diseñada con estructuras horizontales. Los paneles de madera dispuestos longitudinalmente refuerzan la sensación de fluidez y proporcionan ventilación natural. Los techos y los suelos están acabados en madera que aísla acústicamente y absorbe la humedad.

L'abitazione, situata vicino al castello Shizuki e al fiume Hashimoto, sull'isola di Honshu, è stata disegnata tramite strutture orizzontali. I pannelli di legno disposti longitudinalmente rafforzano la sensazione di fluidità e offrono ventilazione naturale. I soffitti e i pavimenti sono rifiniti in legno che isola acusticamente e assorbe l'umidità.

Esta residência, situada perto do castelo de Shizuki e do rio Hashimoto, na ilha de Honshu, foi concebida com base em estruturas horizontais. Os painéis de madeira dispostos longitudinalmente reforçam a sensação de fluidez e proporcionam ventilação natural. Os tetos e pavimentos têm acabamento em madeira, que isola acusticamente e absorve a umidade.

Huset som ligger nära slottet Shizuki och Hashimoto-floden, på ön Honshu, formgavs med horisontella strukturer. Träpaneler arrangerade i längdriktningen förstärker känslan av smidighet och ger naturlig ventilation. Tak och golv med träfinish ljudisolerar och absorberar fukt.

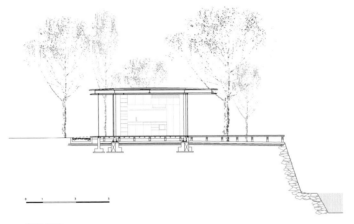

Section / Coupe

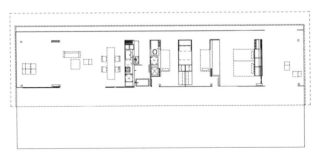

Plan

INSIDE OUT
WOODEN
TOKYO HOUSE

TOKYO, JAPAN
TAKESHI HOSAKA ARCHITECTS
www.hosakatakeshi.com | © Koji Fujii

The shape of the building is an irregular quadrilateral created to fit the irregular quadrangle-shaped plot. The design emphasis was placed on the woodwork and wooden floors, which contrast with the whiteness of the walls. Openings have been made on the sides of the roof and walls to allow sunlight to enter.

Le bâtiment est un quadrilatère irrégulier, qui s'adapte à la situation quadrangulaire de forme irrégulière du lieu. Durant la conception, une grande importance a été accordée à la menuiserie et aux sols en bois qui contrastent avec le blanc des murs. Sur les côtés du toit et les murs du volume, des ouvertures ont été créées pour laisser entrer la lumière du soleil.

Die Form des Gebäudes ist ein unregelmäßiges Viereck, das an den viereckigen, unregelmäßigen Standort angepasst wurde. Beim Design wurde viel Wert auf die Holzarbeiten und die Holzböden gelegt, die mit den weißen Wänden kontrastieren. In die Seiten des Dachs und in die dicken Wände wurden Öffnungen integriert, die den Einfall des Sonnenlichts ermöglichen.

Het gebouw is, in overeenstemming met de onregelmatige vierhoekige ligging, in een onregelmatige vierhoek gebouwd. In het ontwerp is aandacht besteed aan het timmerwerk en de houten vloeren die contrasteren met het wit van de muren. In de zijdelen van het dak en de muren zijn openingen gemaakt waardoor het zonlicht naar binnen kan schijnen.

La forma del edificio es un cuadrilátero irregular que se ajusta a la parcela cuadrangular de forma irregular. En el diseño se dio importancia a la carpintería y los suelos de madera, que contrastan con el blanco de las paredes. En los laterales del techo y las paredes del volumen se han practicado aberturas que permiten la entrada de luz solar.

La forma dell'edificio è un quadrilatero irregolare in sintonia con l'ubicazione quadrangolare a forma irregolare. Nel disegno è stata data importanza ai serramenti e ai pavimenti di legno, in contrasto con il bianco delle pareti. Nelle parti laterali del tetto e nelle pareti del volume sono state praticate delle aperture che consentono l'entrata della luce solare.

A forma do edifício é um quadrilátero irregular, de acordo com o terreno em que está localizado. Neste projeto deu-se grande importância à carpintaria e aos pavimentos em madeira, que contrastam com o branco das paredes. Nas laterais do teto e nas paredes exteriores foram praticadas aberturas que deixam entrar a luz do sol.

Byggnadens form är en oregelbunden fyrhörning som överensstämmer med den oregelbundna fyrsidiga platsen. I designen lades vikt på snickeri och trägolv, som kontrasterar med de vita väggarna. I tak- och väggkanterna har man gjort öppningar som låter solljus komma in.

Site plan / Plan du site

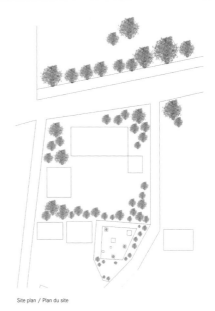

Site plan / Plan du site

Second floor plan / Plan du second niveau

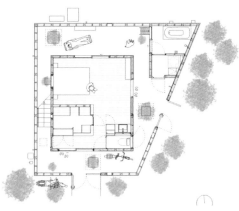

First floor plan / Plan du premier niveau

North elevation / Élévation nord

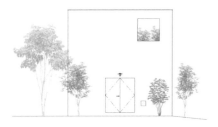

South elevation / Élévation sud

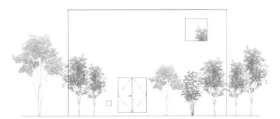

East elevation / Élévation est

West elevation / Élévation ouest

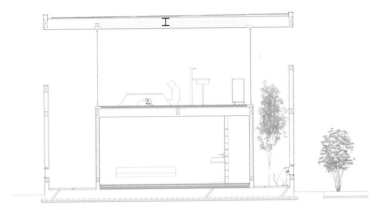

A-A' Section / Coupe A-A'

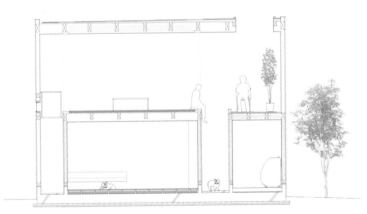

B-B' Section / Coupe B-B'

LEVEL APARTMENT
INSIDE ART NOUVEAU PALACE

LJUBLJANA, SLOVENIA
OFIS ARHITEKTI
www.ofis.si | © Tomaz Gregoric, Jan Celeda

The project is the renovation of an apartment in an Art Nouveau building designed and built by architect Ciril Metod Koch in 1902. The new design features an open space defined by the arrangement of the living rooms at varied heights. The apartment is remarkable for the fusion of the furniture and floor using wood.

Ce projet est une rénovation d'un appartement situé dans un bâtiment de style art nouveau, conçu et construit par l'architecte Ciril Metod Koch en 1902. Le nouveau design propose un espace ouvert défini par la disposition des salles de séjour à différents niveaux. Le bois est utilisé dans la fusion des meubles et du sol pour souligner cette unité.

Renovierungsprojekt eines Apartments in einem *Art Nouveau*-Gebäude, das im Jahre 1902 von dem Architekten Ciril Metod Koch gebaut wurde. Der neue Entwurf berücksichtigt einen offenen Raum, der durch die Anordnung der Wohnräume in verschiedenen Höhen bestimmt wird. Das Holz verbindet die Möbel mit dem Boden, um diese Einheit zu verdeutlichen.

Dit ontwerp ontstond toen een appartement werd gerenoveerd binnen een artnouveaugebouw dat in 1902 werd ontworpen en gebouwd door architect Ciril Metod Koch. In het nieuwe ontwerp wordt de open ruimte bepaald door de verschillende posities van de zitkamers die zich op diverse hoogtes bevinden. Het hout dat is gebruikt in de overgang tussen de meubels en de vloer benadrukt de eenheid tussen de elementen.

El proyecto es la renovación de un apartamento situado en un edificio *art nouveau* diseñado y construido por el arquitecto Ciril Metod Koch en 1902. El nuevo diseño cuenta con un espacio abierto definido por la disposición de las salas de estar en alturas variadas. La madera se utiliza en la fusión de los muebles y el suelo para subrayar esta unidad.

Il progetto consiste nel rinnovamento di un appartamento situato in un edificio *art nouveau* progettato e costruito dall'architetto Ciril Metod Koch nel 1902. Il nuovo progetto presenta uno spazio aperto definito dalla disposizione dei salotti a varie altezze. Il legno è utilizzato nella fusione dei mobili e il pavimento per indicare questa unità.

Este projeto consistiu na renovação de um apartamento situado num edifício arte nova, desenhado e construído pelo arquiteto Ciril Metod Koch, em 1902. O novo *design* conta com um espaço aberto definido pela disposição das salas de estar a diferentes alturas. A madeira é utilizada na fusão dos móveis com o solo, de modo a fazer ressaltar esta unidade.

Projektet är renoveringen av en lägenhet som är belägen i en byggnad i jugendstil som formgavs och byggdes av arkitekten Ciril Metod Koch 1902. Den nya designen har ett öppet utrymme som definieras av vardagsrummen som är placerade på olika nivåer. Virket används i sammansmältningen av möbler och golv för att markera denna enhet.

Sections / Coupes

Plan

1. Entrance / Entrée
2. Living room
3. Kitchen / Cuisine
4. Studio / Atelier
5. Toilet / Toilettes
6. Bathroom / Salle de bains
7. Wardrobe / Garde-robe
8. Bedroom / Chambre
9. Balcony / Balcon

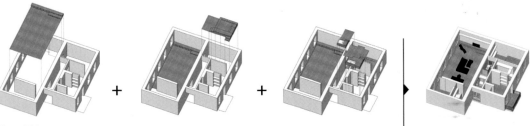

Diagrams / Schémas

Floor level / Niveau du sol

Sideboard level / Niveau de la desserte

Bathroom level / Niveau de la Salle de bains

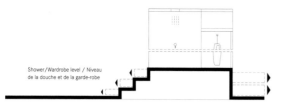
Shower/Wardrobe level / Niveau
de la douche et de la garde-robe

Bedroom level /
Niveau de la chambre

Diagrams / Schémas

THE LUXURIOUS
CELIO APARTMENT

ROME, ITALY
CAROLA VANNINI ARCHITECTURE
www.carolavannini.com | © Stefano Pedretti

In this luxury apartment in central Rome, the direct relationship with the outside area is emphasized by the wooden floor, which extends from the interior to the balcony. The furniture, designed by the same architect, was built in wenge wood, bringing warmth and sobriety to this architectural ensemble.

Dans cet appartement luxueux du centre de Rome, la relation directe avec l'extérieur est soulignée par le sol en bois, qui s'étend de l'intérieur au balcon. Le mobilier créé par le même architecte a été construit en wengé afin d'apporter un aspect chaleureux et sobre à l'ensemble architectural.

In diesem luxuriösen Apartment mitten in Rom, wird der direkte Kontakt mit dem Außenbereich durch den Holzboden betont, der sich vom Innenraum bis zum Balkon erstreckt. Die Möbel, die vom gleichen Architekten entworfen wurden, bestehen aus Wengé-Holz und sollen für Wärme und Nüchternheit in der architektonischen Einheit sorgen.

De directe relatie met het gebied buiten dit luxe appartement in het centrum van Rome wordt benadrukt door de houten vloer, die van de binnenruimte doorloopt in het balkon. Dezelfde architect heeft wengéhout gebruikt voor het door hem ontworpen meubilair, waardoor warmte en soberheid is toegevoegd aan het bouwkundige geheel.

En este lujoso apartamento del centro de Roma, la relación directa con la zona exterior se ve enfatizada por el suelo de madera que se extiende desde el espacio interior al balcón. El mobiliario, diseñado por el mismo arquitecto, fue construido en madera wengé para aportar calidez y sobriedad al conjunto arquitectónico.

In questo lussuoso appartamento nel centro di Roma, il rapporto diretto con l'area esterna è enfatizzato attraverso il pavimento in legno, che si estende dallo spazio interno al balcone. L'arredamento, disegnato dallo stesso architetto, è stato fabbricato in legno wengé per dare calore e sobrietà all'insieme architettonico.

Neste apartamento de luxo situado no centro de Roma, a relação direta com o exterior é enfatizada através do pavimento em madeira, que se estende desde o espaço interior até à varanda. O mobiliário, desenhado pelo mesmo arquiteto, foi fabricado em madeira venguê, conferindo ao conjunto arquitetônico calor e sobriedade.

I denna lyxiga lägenhet i Roms centrum framhävs det direkta förhållandet till området utanför genom golvet av trä, som breder ut sig från insidan till balkongen. Möblemanget som har formgivits av samma arkitekt byggdes med wengé för att tillföra värme och återhållsamhet till den arkitektoniska helheten.

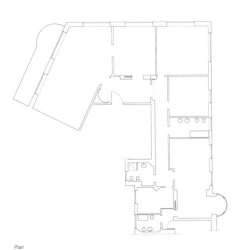

Plan

RESIDENTIAL INTERIORS-EXTERIORS

AMÉNAGEMENTS RÉSIDENTIELS (INTÉRIEURS ET EXTÉRIEURS)

AUSSENGESTALTUNG VON WOHNHÄUSERN

WOONINTERIEURS EN –EXTERIEURS

INTERIORES-EXTERIORES RESIDENCIALES

INTERNI/ESTERNI AD USO ABITATIVO

INTERIORES/EXTERIORES RESIDENCIAIS

BOSTADSINTERIÖRER OCH EXTERIÖRER

LE NUAGE REFUGE
FOR THE PARC DES COTEAUX

LORMONT, FRANCE
BRUIT DU FRIGO
www.bruitdufrigo.com | © Bruit du Frigo

This small house or shelter for up to 5 or 8 people has a design similar to a cloud. This original form pays homage to the utopian architecture and radical design of the 60's and 70's, reminiscent of caravan kitsch. Constructed of wood, its curved forms contrast with the inclined straight lines of the windows.

Cette petite construction, ou refuge, pouvant accueillir 5 à 8 personnes ressemble à un nuage. Cette forme originale rend hommage à l'architecture utopique et au design radical des années 60 et 70, aux réminiscences kitsch des caravanes. Construite en bois, ses courbes contrastent avec les lignes droites et inclinées des fenêtres.

Dieses kleine Wohnhaus oder Berghütte, in dem fünf bis acht Personen untergebracht werden können, erinnert durch seine Gestaltung an eine Wolke. Diese außergewöhnliche Form ist eine Huldigung an die utopische Architektur und das radikale Design der 60er und 70er Jahre und erinnert an den Wohnwagen-Kitsch. Es ist vollständig aus Holz gebaut und seine kurvigen Formen kontrastieren mit den geraden, geneigten Linien der Fenster.

Deze kleine woning of tijdelijk onderkomen biedt onderdak aan 5 tot 8 personen. Ze is ontworpen in de vorm van een wolk. De originele vorm is een eerbetoon aan de utopische architectuur en het Radical Design van de jaren '60 en '70 van de vorige eeuw, en doet denken aan de wat kitscherige caravans. De constructie met kromme vormen contrasteert met de schuin lopende rechte lijnen van de ramen.

Esta pequeña vivienda o refugio con capacidad para 5 y 8 personas tiene un diseño semejante a una nube. Esta original forma rinde homenaje a la arquitectura utópica y el diseño radical de los años sesenta y setenta, reminiscencias *kitsch* de las caravanas. Construida en madera, sus formas curvas contrastan con las líneas rectas inclinadas de las ventanas.

Questa piccola abitazione o rifugio che può ospitare 5 o 8 persone ha un design simile ad una nuvola. Questa forma originale rende omaggio all'architettura utopica e al design radicale degli anni '60 e '70, reminiscenze *kitsch* dei caravan. Costruita in legno, le sue forme curve contrastano con le linee rette inclinate delle finestre.

Este pequeno bangalô ou abrigo, com capacidade para 5 a 8 pessoas, tem uma forma semelhante a uma nuvem. Com esta forma tão singular pretende-se prestar homenagem à arquitetura utópica e ao design radical dos anos 60 e 70, uma reminiscência *kitsch* das caravanas. Construída em madeira, as suas formas arredondadas contrastam com as linhas retas inclinadas das janelas.

Detta lilla hem eller tillflyktsort med plats för 5 till 8 personer, har en design som liknar ett moln. Denna nyskapande form hyllar utopisk arkitektur och den radikala designen på 60- och 70-talet, drag som vagt erinrar om husvagnskitsch. Det är byggt i trä och dess böjda former utgör en kontrast mot de raka linjerna som utgår ifrån fönstren.

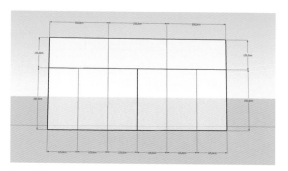

Sections / Coupes

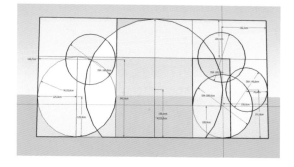

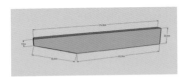

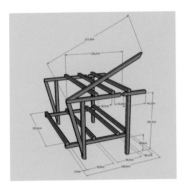

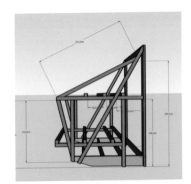

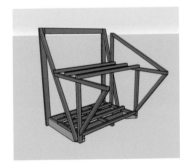

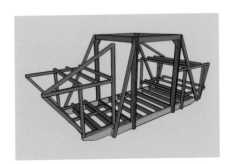

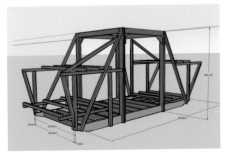

Diagrams / Schémas

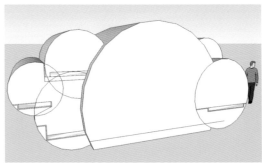

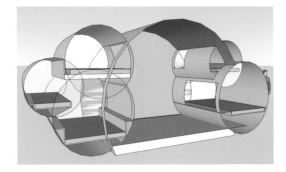

Diagrams / Schémas

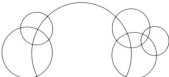

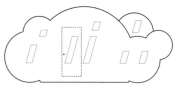
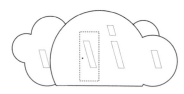

Schema / Schémas

SINGLE FAMILY
HOUSE VILLA D

STOCKHOLM, SWEDEN
RB ARKITEKTUR
www.rbarkitektur.se | © Ulrika Ekblom

The striking feature of the project is in its position on a rock. The client's wish was to have the access point as high as possible, so as to obtain a panoramic view of the landscape. The rectangular building is built into the rock and supported by a cantilever. The wooden panelling was stained grey to harmonize with nature.

L'originalité du projet réside dans sa position sur un rocher. Le client souhaitait accéder au point le plus haut afin d'avoir une vue panoramique du paysage. La construction de forme rectangulaire s'intègre dans la roche et se projette en saillie. Le revêtement des panneaux de bois a été teint en gris par souci d'harmonie avec la nature.

Die Originalität des Projekts entsteht durch die Position des Gebäudes auf einem Felsen. Der Kunde wollte den höchsten Punkt des Standorts erreichen, um von dort aus den Panoramablick auf die Landschaft zu genießen. Die Bebauung in rechteckiger Form wurde in den Felsen integriert, mit eingeplantem Vorsprung. Die Verkleidung aus Holzpaneelen wurde grau eingefärbt, sodass sie mit der Natur harmonisiert.

Wat dit ontwerp origineel maakt, is dat het is gebouwd op een rots. De opdrachtgever wenste dat het op het hoogste punt zou komen te staan, vanwege het panoramische uitzicht op het landschap. Het rechthoekige bouwwerk is geïntegreerd in de rots en benadrukt met een vooruitstekend deel. De houten deklaag is grijs geverfd zodat het een harmonisch geheel vormt met de natuur.

La originalidad del proyecto estriba en su posición sobre una roca. El deseo del cliente era acceder al punto más alto del lugar para conseguir una visión panorámica del paisaje. La edificación de forma rectangular se integra a la roca y se proyecta en voladizo. El revestimiento de paneles de madera se tintó de gris para armonizar con la naturaleza.

L'originalità del progetto deriva dalla sua posizione su di una roccia. Il desiderio del cliente era quello di accedere al punto più alto del luogo, con l'obiettivo di ottenere una vista panoramica del paesaggio. La costruzione a forma rettangolare è integrata nella roccia e progettata a sbalzo. Il rivestimento in pannelli di legno è stato tinto di grigio per adattarsi alla natura.

A originalidade deste projeto reside na sua posição sobre uma rocha. O desejo do cliente era aceder ao ponto mais alto do lugar para uma visão panorâmica da paisagem. O edifício, de forma retangular, está integrado na rocha e é projetado formando um telheiro. O revestimento com painéis de madeira foi pintado de cinzento para se harmonizar com a natureza.

Originaliteten i projektet ligger i dess läge på en klippa. Kunden ville få tillgång till den högsta punkten på platsen, med syftet att få en panoramavy över landskapet. Den rektangulärt formade byggnaden har inlemmats i berget och har ett utsprång. Väggbeklädnaden i trä målades grå för att vara i harmoni med naturen.

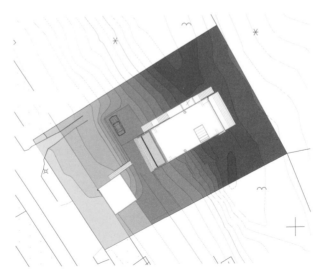

Site plan / Plan du site

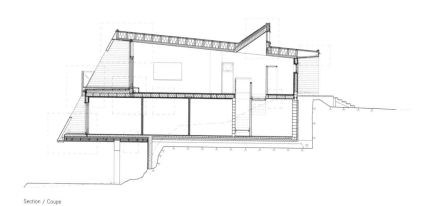

Section / Coupe

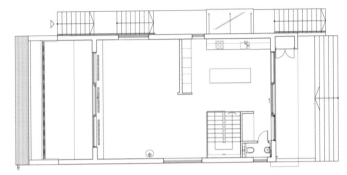

Second floor plan / Plan du second niveau

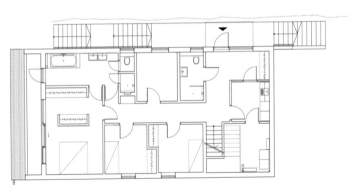

First floor plan / Plan du premier niveau

FINNISH COTTAGE
FOUR-CORNERED VILLA

VIRRAT, FINLAND
AVANTO ARCHITECTS
www.avan.to / © Anders Portman, Martin Sommerschield / kuvio.com

The basic idea of this project is to provide an example of a sustainable home in contrast with typical Finnish cottages. The building is well insulated, with sunlight and no running water. The cross shaped floor plan provides for four different viewing points. The black exterior of local wood contrasts with the lighter colours of the interior.

L'idée de base de ce projet est de donner un exemple de maison durable qui contraste avec les cabanes finlandaises caractéristiques. La construction est bien isolée, sans eau courante et avec la lumière du soleil. Le plan en croix permet d'avoir quatre points de vue différents. L'extérieur en bois local de couleur noire contraste avec l'intérieur aux couleurs plus claires.

Die Grundidee dieses Projekts war, ein Beispiel für ein nachhaltiges Haus zu geben, das sich von den typischen finnländischen Hütten abhebt. Der Bau liegt ziemlich abgelegen, hat kein fließendes Wasser und wird mit Solarenergie versorgt. Die kreuzförmige Etage bietet vier verschiedene Aussichtspunkte. Der Außenbereich wurde aus dem vor Ort vorkommenden schwarzen Holz gestaltet und kontrastiert mit den helleren Farben des Innenraums.

De architecten van dit ontwerp hebben een voorbeeld willen geven van een huis dat, anders dan de meeste Finse houten hutten, duurzaam is. Het gebouw ligt erg afgelegen, het heeft geen stromend water en alleen zonne-energie. Doordat het in een kruisvorm is gebouwd zijn er vier verschillende uitzichten. De buitenzijde van lokaal zwartgebeitst hout contrasteert met de lichte kleuren van het interieur.

La idea básica de este proyecto es proporcionar un ejemplo de casa sostenible en contraste con las típicas cabañas finlandesas. La construcción está bien aislada, no dispone de agua corriente y se ilumina con luz solar. La planta en cruz permite tener cuatro puntos de vista diferentes. El exterior de madera local de color negro contrasta con la del interior, de colores más claros.

L'idea fondamentale di questo progetto è quella di offrire un esempio di casa sostenibile in contrasto con le tipiche capanne finlandesi. La costruzione è ben isolata, senza acqua corrente e con luce solare. La pianta a croce permette di avere quattro diversi punti di vista. La parte esterna in legno locale di colore nero contrasta con quella degli interni, di colori più chiari.

A ideia básica deste projeto foi criar um exemplo de casa sustentável, seguindo o modelo das cabanas finlandesas típicas. A construção está bem isolada, sem água corrente e com luz solar. A planta em cruz permite quatro pontos de vista diferentes. O exterior, de madeira negra, contrasta com o interior, de cores muito claras.

Den grundläggande idén med projektet är att ge ett exempel på hållbarhet inom boende i motsats till typiska finländska stugor. Konstruktionen är väl isolerad utan rinnande vatten och med solljus. En planlösning i form av ett kryss gör att man kan se åt fyra olika håll. Utsidan med lokalt trä i svart färg kontrasterar mot de ljusare färgerna inuti.

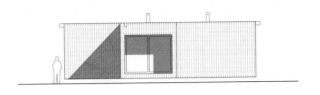

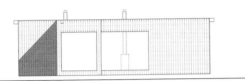

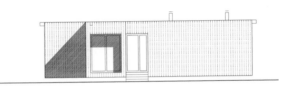

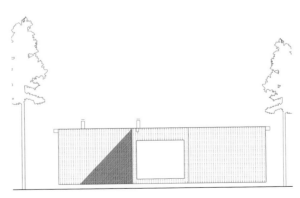

Elevations / Élévations

Plan

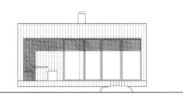

East elevation / Élévation est

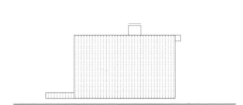

North elevation / Élévation nord

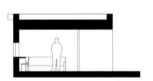

Section A-A' / Coupe A-A'

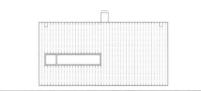

West elevation / Élévation ouest

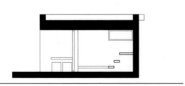

Section B-B' / Coupe B-B'

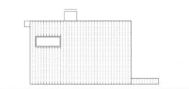

South elevation / Élévation sud

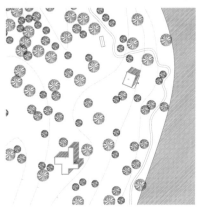

Site plan / Plan du site

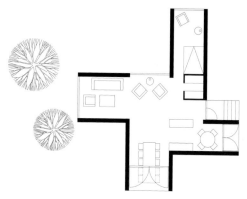

Plan

1940'S RENOVATION
RESIDENCE 1414

AUSTIN, TX, USA
MIRÓ RIVERA ARCHITECTS
www.mirorivera.com | © Miró Rivera Architects

The project was to renovate a house built in 1940 with an extension added in 1980. The main process was to open up the house to let in more light. Among the materials used, wood stands out, being used extensively in the interior and exterior for flooring, handrails, kitchen islands, worktops, ceilings, etc..

Ce projet est une rénovation d'une maison construite en 1940 avec une annexe ajoutée en 1980. La principale intervention a consisté à ouvrir la maison pour laisser entrer la lumière. Parmi les matériaux utilisés, le bois a été employé en abondance à l'intérieur et à l'extérieur : sols, rampes, îlots de cuisine, comptoirs, toits, etc.

Ziel des Projekts war die Renovierung eines Hauses aus dem Jahr 1940, mit einem Anbau, der 1980 hinzugefügt wurde. Das Wichtigste bei der Planung war die Öffnung des Hauses, um mehr Licht hineinzulassen. Von den verwendeten Materialien fällt besonders das Holz auf, das großzügig im Innen- und Außenbereich verwendet wurde, wie beispielsweise für Fußböden, Handläufe, Kochinseln, Theken, Decken usw.

Dit ontwerp is tot stand gekomen met de renovatie van een huis uit 1940 dat in 1980 werd uitgebreid. De belangrijkste verandering is dat het huis opener is geworden waardoor er meer licht binnenvalt. Van de gebruikte materialen valt het hout het meest op. Er is zowel binnen als buiten ruimschoots gebruik van gemaakt: in de vloeren, leuningen, kookeilanden, balies, plafonds, etc.

El proyecto consistió en la renovación de una casa construida en 1940 y con un anexo construido en 1980. La actuación principal fue la apertura de la casa para dejar entrar más luz. De entre los materiales utilizados destaca la madera, que se emplea ampliamente en el interior y el exterior: suelos, pasamanos, islas de cocina, mostradores, techos, etc.

Il progetto si è basato sulla ristrutturazione di una casa costruita nel 1940 con un ampliamento realizzato nel 1980. L'azione principale è stata l'apertura della casa per permettere che entrasse più luce. Tra i materiali impiegati si distingue il legno, utilizzato ampiamente negli interni ed esterni: pavimenti, corrimani, isole da cucina, banconi, tetti, etc.

Este projeto consistiu na remodelação de uma casa construída em 1940 com uma ampliação acrescentada em 1980. A principal intervenção foi a abertura da casa, para deixar entrar mais luz. Entre os materiais utilizados destaca-se a madeira, generosamente utilizada tanto no exterior como no interior: pavimentos, corrimões, ilhas de cozinha, bancadas, tetos, etc.

Projektet bestod av renoveringen av ett hus som byggdes 1940 med en tillbyggnad gjord 1980. Den största åtgärden var att öppna upp huset för större ljusinsläpp. Mest framträdande av materialen som använts är trä, som använts flitigt såväl på ut- som insidan: golv, ledstänger, köksöar, bänkskåp, tak, mm.

Elevation / Élévation

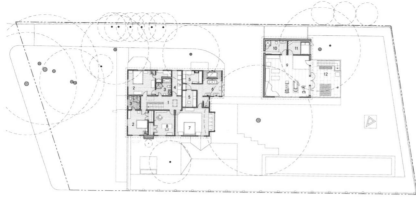

Second floor plan / Plan du second niveau

1. Hall
2. Bedroom / Chambre
3. Bathroom / Salle de bains
4. Laundry / Buanderie
5. Master Closet / Cabinet principal
6. Master Bathroom / Salle de bains principale
7. Master Bedroom / Chambre principale
8. Office / Bureau
9. Gym / Salle de sport
10. Guest Bathroom / Salle de bains pour invités
11. Guest Bedroom / Chambre d'amis
12. Gym Deck / Annexe de la salle de sport

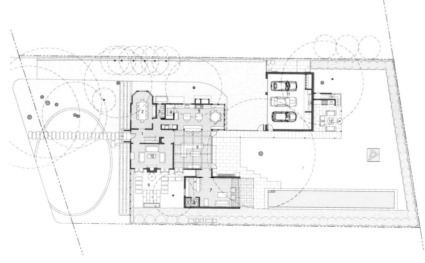

First floor plan / Plan du premier niveau

1. Entry / Entrée
2. Dining / Salle à manger
3. Powder Bath / Salle de bains
4. Pantry / Garde-manger
5. Kitchen/Breakfast / Cuisine
6. Family Room / Salle de séjour
7. Den / Salon
8. Pool Bath / Salle de bains
9. Sideyard Patio / Terrasse latérale
10. Living Room
11. Garage
12. Backyard Patio / Terrasse arrière

HOUSE AT
LAKE CONSTANCE
IN AUSTRIA

LAKE CONSTANCE, AUSTRIA
N-V-O ARCHITECTS, JÜRGEN STOPPEL
www.n-v-o.com | © Günter Laznia/N-V-O Architects, Jürgen Stoppel

The house, built entirely of wood, consists of a simple cube shape, two balconies and entrance area. The larch panelling creates a dialogue with the fruit trees surrounding the house. The wood confers a certain elegance upon the environment emphasized by furniture and openings that provide natural light.

L'habitation, entièrement construite en bois, se compose d'un volume cubique simple, de deux balcons et d'une zone d'entrée. Le revêtement en bois de mélèze établit un dialogue avec les arbres fruitiers qui entourent l'habitation. Le bois confère à l'environnement une élégance, soulignée par le mobilier et les ouvertures qui apportent la lumière naturelle.

Die Wohnung, die vollständig aus Holz gebaut wurde, besteht aus einem einfachen würfelförmigen Raum, zwei Balkonen und einem Eingangsbereich. Die Täfelung aus Lerchenholz stellt einen Dialog mit den Obstbäumen her, welche die Wohnung umgeben. Das Holz verleiht der Umgebung, durch die Möbel und die Öffnungen, eine nachdrückliche Eleganz. Letztere sorgen für den Einfall natürlichen Lichts.

Deze volledig uit hout opgetrokken woning bestaat uit een eenvoudige kubusvorm, twee balkons en een entreegedeelte. Door de larikshouten bekleding ontstaat als het ware een tweespraak met de fruitbomen rondom het huis. Door het gebruik van hout krijgt de omgeving een elegante uitstraling die nog eens wordt benadrukt door het meubiliar en de openingen waardoor natuurlijk licht naar binnen schijnt.

La vivienda, construida íntegramente en madera, se compone de un volumen cúbico simple, dos balcones y una zona de entrada. El revestimiento de madera de alerce establece un diálogo con los árboles frutales que rodean la vivienda. La madera confiere al entorno una elegancia enfatizada por el mobiliario y las aberturas que proporcionan luz natural.

L'edificio, costruito interamente in legno, è composto da un volume cubico semplice, due balconi e una zona di accesso. Il rivestimento in legno di larice stabilisce un dialogo con gli alberi da frutta che circondano l'abitazione. Il legno attribuisce all'ambiente un'eleganza accentuata dall'arredamento e dalle aperture che permettono alla luce naturale di entrare.

Esta casa, construída integralmente em madeira, é constituída por um volume cúbico simples, duas varandas e uma zona de entrada. O revestimento em madeira de larício estabelece um diálogo com as árvores de fruto que rodeiam a casa. A madeira confere ao conjunto uma elegância sublinhada pelo mobiliário e as aberturas que proporcionam luz natural.

Bostadshuset, byggt helt i trä, består av ett enkelt kubiskt utrymme, två balkonger och ett ingångsområde. Lärkträdsfodringen upprättar en dialog med fruktträden som omger huset. Träet ger miljön en elegans som understryks av möblemanget och öppningarna som ger dagsljus.

Section / Coupe

Lower level / Niveau inférieur

JAMES ROBERTSON HOUSE
IN MacKERAL BEACH

GREAT MacKERAL BEACH, AUSTRALIA
CASEY BROWN ARCHITECTURE
www.caseybrown.com.au | © Anthony Browell, Patrick Bingham Hall, Elliot Cohen

The project consists of two pavilions for a couple. The project aims to make the most of the outdoor spaces and to divide the house into two units. Various types of wood have been used for the interior and exterior walkways to satisfy the requirements of the architects, who wished to integrate the house with the landscape.

Le projet se compose de deux pavillons destinés à un couple. L'objectif est de profiter au maximum des espaces extérieurs et de diviser la maison en deux unités. L'utilisation des différents types de bois, tant à l'intérieur que sur les passerelles extérieures, répond à la volonté des architectes d'intégrer la maison dans le paysage.

Das Projekt besteht aus zwei Pavillons, die für ein Ehepaar gedacht sind. Das Projekt versucht die Außenräume optimal zu nutzen und das Haus in zwei Einheiten zu unterteilen. Die Verwendung unterschiedlicher Holzarten, sowohl im Innenraum als auch bei den äußeren Stegen, entspricht dem Wunsch der Architekten, das Haus in die Landschaft zu integrieren.

Dit ontwerp bestaat uit twee paviljoens die zijn bestemd voor één stel. Het huis is in twee eenheden opgedeeld en er is getracht maximaal profijt te trekken van de buitenruimten. Met het gebruik van verschillende soorten hout, voor zowel het interieur als voor de buitenvlonder, hebben de architecten ernaar gestreefd het huis deel te laten worden van het landschap.

El proyecto se compone de dos pabellones destinados a una pareja. El proyecto busca aprovechar al máximo los espacios exteriores y dividir la casa en dos unidades. La utilización de diferentes tipos de madera tanto en el interior como en las pasarelas exteriores responde a la voluntad de los arquitectos de integrar la casa en el paisaje.

Il progetto è composto da due padiglioni destinati a una coppia. Il progetto cerca di approfittare al massimo degli spazi esterni e dividere la casa in due unità. L'uso di diversi tipi di legno, sia all'interno sia per le passerelle esterne, risponde alla volontà degli architetti di integrare la casa nel paesaggio.

Este projeto é constituído por dois pavilhões, destinados a um casal. A ideia foi aproveitar ao máximo os espaços exteriores e dividir a casa em duas unidades. O uso de diversos tipos de madeira, tanto no interior como nos passadiços exteriores, obedece à vontade de integração da casa na paisagem por parte dos arquitetos.

Projektet består av två paviljonger avsedda för ett par. Projektet försöker utnyttja maximalt de yttre utrymmena och indela huset i två enheter. Användning av olika typer av trä, både inomhus och på de yttre gångbroarna, motsvarar arkitekternas önskan om att integrera huset i landskapet.

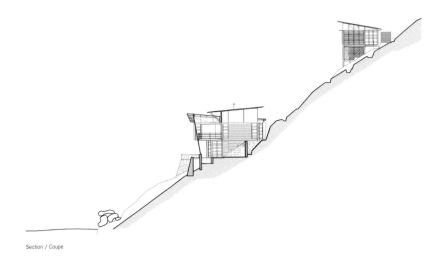

Section / Coupe

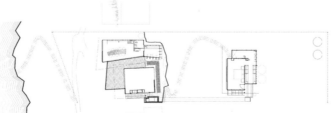

Ground floor plan / Plan du rez-de-chaussée

Basement floor / Plan du sous-sol

TROPICAL HOUSE IN
MUNDAÚ-CEARÁ

MUNDAÚ, BRAZIL
CAMARIM ARCHITECTS
www.camarim.pt | © Nic Olshiati

The clients requested a holiday home that would allow ample opportunity for contact with nature. The architects built a wooden skin to cover the structure, priority being given to the top of the house. For the construction, they hired local carpenters with extensive experience in using local techniques and materials.

Les clients souhaitaient une maison de vacances offrant de nombreuses possibilités de contact avec la nature. Les architectes ont recouvert toute la structure d'un manteau de bois, notamment dans la partie supérieure de l'habitation. À cet effet, on a engagé des menuisiers de la région qui ont une grande expérience des techniques et des matériaux locaux.

Die Kunden verlangten ein Ferienhaus, das viele Möglichkeiten für den Kontakt mit der Natur bieten sollte. Die Architekten bauten eine Holzhaut, welche die Struktur umgibt, was hauptsächlich für den oberen Teil des Wohnhauses gilt. Für die Bauausführung wurden lokal ansässige Tischler beauftragt, die über umfassende Erfahrung mit den Techniken und bodenständigen Materialien verfügen.

De opdrachtgevers vroegen om een vakantiehuis dat uitgebreide mogelijkheden biedt om in contact te staan met de natuur. De architecten ontwierpen een houten bedekking om het raamwerk, vooral om het bovenste deel van de woning. Voor de bouw zijn lokale timmerlieden in dienst genomen die beschikken over uitgebreide ervaring en kennis van de inheemse materialen.

Los clientes demandaban una casa de vacaciones que permitieran amplias posibilidades de contacto con la naturaleza. Los arquitectos construyeron una piel de madera que envuelve la estructura, sobre todo en la parte superior de la vivienda. En la construcción se trabajó con carpinteros locales con amplia experiencia en técnicas y materiales del lugar.

I clienti richiedevano una casa di vacanza che concedesse ampie possibilità di contatto con la natura. Gli architetti hanno costruito un involucro di legno che ricopre la struttura, soprattutto nella parte superiore dell'abitazione. Per la costruzione sono stati impiegati falegnami locali dotati di vasta esperienza nelle tecniche e nei materiali autoctoni.

Os clientes pretendiam uma casa de férias que permitisse amplas possibilidades de contato com a natureza. Os arquitetos construíram uma pele de madeira que envolve toda a estrutura, sobretudo na parte superior da casa. Para a sua construção foram contratados carpinteiros locais, com vasta experiência nas técnicas e materiais autóctones.

Kunderna ville ha ett fritidshus som ger många möjligheter till kontakt med naturen. Arkitekterna byggde ett hölje av trä som omger byggnaden, framför allt i den övre delen av huset. För dess konstruktion rekryterades lokala snickare med omfattande erfarenhet av inhemska metoder och material.

Site plan / Plan du site

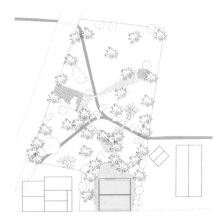

Plan

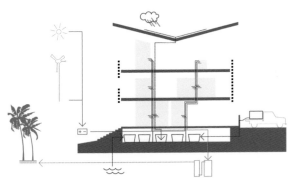

Diagram / Schéma

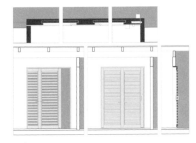

Elevation / Élévation

291

Third floor plan / Plan du troisième niveau

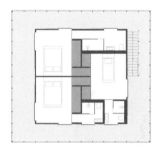

Second floor plan / Plan du deuxième niveau

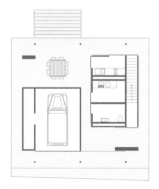

First floor plan / Plan du premier niveau

LITTLE BLACK DRESS
A HOUSE LIKE A SHADOW

GUNSKIRCHEN, AUSTRIA
X ARCHITEKTEN
www.xarchitekten.com | © Rupert Asanger, Kurt Hörbst

The project was designed to provide a private residence to a young couple. The design was based on the typical local farms of the area, reinterpreting the classic form of a gabled roof, a patio and a monolithic annex. The white wood used is outstanding, contrasting with the dark covering of the building.

Le projet concernait une résidence privée destinée à un jeune couple. Sa conception s'est basée sur la typologie locale des fermes voisines, en réinterprétant la forme classique de toiture à deux pentes, un patio et un bâtiment annexe monolithique. Sa caractéristique réside dans l'utilisation du bois blanc qui contraste avec le revêtement sombre du bâtiment.

Dieses Projekt wurde konzipiert, um den privaten Wohnsitz für ein junges Paar zu beherbergen. Das Design basiert auf der lokalen Typologie der nahe gelegenen Bauernhöfe, wobei für das Satteldach, den Innenhof und einen monolithischen Anbau des Gebäudes, die klassischen Formen neuinterpretiert wurden. Charakteristisch ist das weiße Holz, das verwendet wurde, da es mit der dunklen Ummantelung des Gebäudes kontrastierte.

Dit gebouw is ontworpen als privéwoning voor een jong stel. Het ontwerp is geïnspireerd op de typerende indeling van de naburige boerderijen. Het dak heeft een klassieke vorm die bestaat uit twee hellende vlakken, er is een binnenplaats en een monolitisch bijgebouw. Kenmerkend is het gebruik van wit hout dat contrasteert met de donkere kleur van de buitenzijde.

El proyecto fue creado para convetirse en una residencia privada de una pareja joven. El diseño se basó en la tipología local de las granjas vecinas, reinterpretando la forma clásica de cubierta a dos aguas, un patio y un edificio anexo monolítico. Es característica la madera blanca utilizada que contrasta con el obscuro envoltorio del edificio.

Il progetto fu ideato per ospitare una residenza destinata a una giovane coppia. Il design fu impostato sulla tipologia locale delle vicine fattorie, reinterpretando la classica forma di tetto a due falde, un cortile e un edificio monolitico annesso. È caratteristico il legno bianco utilizzato, che contrasta con l'involucro scuro dell'edificio.

Este projeto foi criado para albergar uma residência privada, destinada a um casal jovem. O design inspira-se na tipologia local das quintas vizinhas, reinterpretando a forma clássica, com telhado de duas águas, um pátio e um edifício anexo monolítico. É muito característica a utilização da madeira branca, que contrasta com o revestimento escuro do edifício.

Projektet utformades för att ge plats åt en privatbostad för ett ungt par. Formen byggde på de närliggande bondgårdarnas lokala stil, med en nygestaltning av den klassiska formen med två taksidor, en uteplats och en monolitisk tillbyggnad. Det ljusa träet som används är utmärkande, vilket kontrasterar med byggnadens mörka hölje.

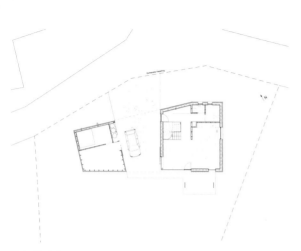

Site plan / Plan du site

Elevations / Élévations

Elevations / Élévations

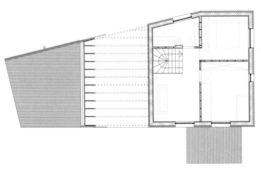

Plan

LA LUGE
IN LA CONCEPTION-LAURENTIDES

LA CONCEPTION-LAURENTIDES, CANADA
**MARIE-CLAUDE HAMELIN, LOUKAS YIACOUVAKIS,
JULIE LAROUCHE / YIACOUVAKIS HAMELIN ARCHITECTES**
www.yh2architecture.com | © Francis Pelletier

This small but long house is located in a woodland belonging to the municipality of La Conception. The architects chose wood as the ideal material to integrate the house with the natural environment, to absorb moisture, retain warmth and provide the comfort requested by the customers.

Cette petite habitation de structure longitudinale est située sur un terrain boisé appartenant à la municipalité de La Conception. Les architectes ont choisi le bois pour intégrer la maison dans la nature, absorber l'humidité, garder la chaleur et apporter le confort que souhaitaient les clients.

Dieses kleine Wohnhaus mit einer länglichen Struktur befindet sich in einem bewaldeten Gebiet, das zur Gemeinde La Conception gehört. Die Architekten entschieden sich für Holz als geeignetes Material, um das Haus in die Natur zu integrieren, um Feuchtigkeit zu absorbieren, Wärme zu speichern und für die Behaglichkeit zu sorgen, die sich die Kunden wünschten.

Deze kleine, in de lengte ontworpen woning staat op een bosrijk terrein binnen de gemeente La Conception. De architecten hebben gekozen voor hout omdat dat als materiaal geschikt is om het huis met de natuur te laten integreren, omdat het vocht opneemt en de warmte vasthoudt en omdat het voldoet aan het comfort waar de opdrachtgevers om vroegen.

Esta pequeña vivienda de estructura longitudinal se sitúa en un terreno boscoso perteneciente a la municipalidad de La Conception. Los arquitectos seleccionaron la madera como el material idóneo para integrar la casa con la naturaleza, absorber la humedad, mantener el calor y aportar el confort que deseaban los clientes.

Questa piccola abitazione dalla struttura longitudinale è situata in un terreno boscoso che appartiene al comune di La Conception. Gli architetti hanno scelto il legno come materiale adatto a inserire la casa nella natura, assorbire l'umidità, mantenere il calore e offrire il comfort ricercato dai clienti.

Esta pequena residência de estrutura longitudinal fica situada num terreno arborizado, no município de La Conception. Os arquitetos selecionaram a madeira como material mais adequado para integrar a casa na natureza, absorver a umidade, conservar o calor e proporcionar o conforto exigido pelos clientes.

Detta lilla hus med längsgående struktur är beläget i ett trädbevuxet område som tillhör kommunen La Conception. Arkitekterna valde trä som det perfekta materialet att integrera huset i naturen, absorbera fukt, hålla värmen och bidra med den bekvämlighet som kunderna ville ha.

HOUSE IN
STOCKHOLM ARCHIPELAGO

STOCKHOLM ARCHIPELAGO, SWEDEN
THAM & VIDEGÅRD ARKITEKTER
www.tvark.se | © Lindman Photography

The starting point of this project was to establish a direct relationship with the spectacular scenery of the archipelago. The house was designed as a lightweight construction of wood and glass. The wood provided simplicity of construction at a low cost, and was also stained black to create a connection with the tall pines of the island and the Baltic Sea.

Le point de départ de ce projet consistait à établir une relation directe avec le paysage spectaculaire de l'archipel. L'habitation a été conçue comme une construction légère en bois et en verre. Le bois offrait une facilité de construction et un faible coût. Il a été peint en noir pour se fondre aux sapins de l'île et la mer Baltique.

Der Ausgangspunkt dieses Projekts war die Herstellung einer direkten Beziehung zur spektakulären Landschaft des Archipels. Das Wohnhaus wurde als eine leichte Konstruktion aus Holz und Glas konzipiert. Das Holz sorgt für eine einfache Bauweise und niedrige Kosten, außerdem wurde es schwarz eingefärbt, um die Verbindung mit den hohen Kiefern der Insel und dem baltischen Meere herzustellen.

Het spectaculaire landschap van de Finse archipel vormde het uitgangspunt voor dit ontwerp. De woning bestaat uit een lichte constructie van hout en glas. Door het gebruik van hout is het ontwerp eenvoudig en goedkoop. Het gebouw is donker geschilderd om een relatie te leggen met de hoge pijnbomen die op het eiland staan en de omringende Baltische Zee.

El punto de partida de este proyecto era proporcionar una relación directa con el paisaje espectacular del archipiélago. La vivienda fue concebida como una construcción ligera en madera y vidrio. La madera proporcionó simplicidad de construcción y bajo coste, además fue teñida de negro para vincularla con los altos pinos de la isla y el mar Báltico.

Il punto di partenza di questo progetto era stabilire un rapporto diretto con il paesaggio spettacolare dell'arcipelago. L'abitazione fu concepita come una costruzione leggera di legno e vetro. Il legno ha offerto facilità di costruzione e bassi costi, inoltre è stata tinta di nero per associarla agli alti pini dell'isola e al mar Baltico.

O ponto de partida deste projeto foi o estabelecimento de uma relação direta com a paisagem espetacular do arquipélago. A casa foi concebida como uma construção ligeira de madeira e vidro. A simplicidade e baixo custo da construção ficaram-se a dever à utilização de madeira, que foi depois pintada de negro para a relacionar com os altos pinheiros da ilha e com o mar Báltico.

Utgångspunkten för detta projekt var att upprätta ett direkt samband med skärgårdens spektakulära landskap. Huset var tänkt som en lätt konstruktion av trä och glas. Med trä kunde uppförandet bli enkelt och kostnadseffektivt, och det målades i svart ton för att koppla ihop det med öns höga tallar och Östersjön.

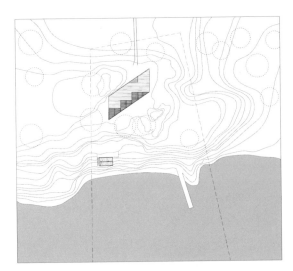

Site plan / Plan du site

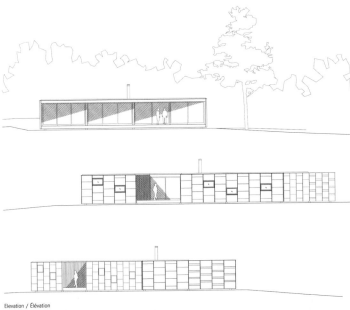

Elevation / Élévation

Plan

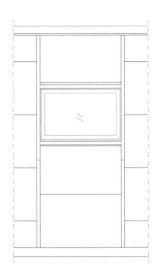

Facade Section / Coupe de la façade

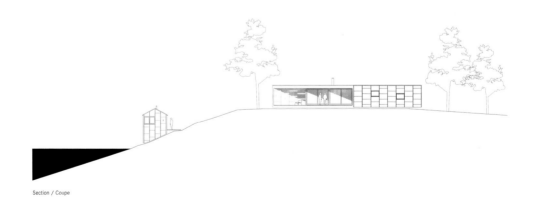

Section / Coupe

GULF ISLANDS
RESIDENCE & BOAT HOUSE

SALT SPRING ISLAND, CANADA
RURAL URBAN FANTASY PROJECT
www.rufproject.com | © Ivan Hunter

The client asked for a private residence that would combine the concepts of the typical Canadian rustic log cabin and a glass house. The architects created a structure with large expanses of glass using a simple and minimal palette featuring local wood, hemlock, Alaska spruce and yellow cedar for the exterior.

Le client demandait une résidence privée qui associerait le concept de cabane en bois rustique, caractéristique du Canada, à une petite maison de verre. Les architectes ont créé une structure avec de grandes extensions en verre et une palette de matériaux simples et minimalistes avec du bois local, le tsuga, les sapins d'Alaska et le cèdre jaune à l'extérieur.

Der Kunde wünschte ein privates Wohnhaus, welches das Konzept der rustikalen, typisch kanadischen Holzhütten mit einem Glashäuschen vereint. Die Architekten schufen eine Struktur mit großen gläsernen Flächen und verwendeten eine Reihe von einfachen minimalistischen Materialien. Allen voran heimische Holzarten wie Schierling, Tannen aus Alaska und gelbe Zeder für den Außenbereich.

De opdrachtgever wenste een privéwoning waarin het concept van een typisch Canadese houten plattelandshut zou worden samengevoegd met het ontwerp van een glazen huis. Daarop creëerden de architecten een gebouw met grote glazen puien en een keuze aan eenvoudige en minimalistische materialen, in het bijzonder lokaal hout, scheerling, Alaska-sparren en gele ceder voor het exterieur.

El cliente demandaba una residencia privada que aunara la idea de cabaña de madera rústica típica de Canadá y una casita de cristal. Los arquitectos crearon una estructura con grandes extensiones de vidrio y una paleta de materiales simples y mínimos capitaneados por la madera local, la cicuta, los abetos de Alaska y el cedro amarillo en el exterior.

Il cliente ricercava una residenza privata che riunisse il concetto di capanna di legno rustica tipica del Canada e una casetta di vetro. Gli architetti hanno creato una struttura con grandi superfici di vetro e una gamma di materiali semplici e minimalisti capitanati dal legno locale, la cicuta, gli abeti dell'Alaska e il cedro giallo sull'esterno.

O cliente pretendia uma residência privada que conjugasse o conceito de cabana de madeira rústica típica do Canadá com o de uma casinha de vidro. Os arquitetos criaram uma estrutura com grandes extensões de vidro e uma paleta de materiais simples e mínimos, liderada pelas madeiras locais, cicuta, abeto-do-alasca e cedro-amarelo no exterior.

Kunden ville ha en privatbostad som skulle föra egenskaperna för en lantlig trästuga typisk för Kanada och ett litet hus av glas. Arkitekterna skapade en struktur med stora glaspartier och en palett av enkla och minimala material lett av lokalt trä, odört, Alaska-gran och gult cederträ på utsidan.

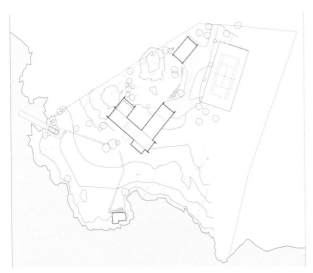

Site plan / Plan du site

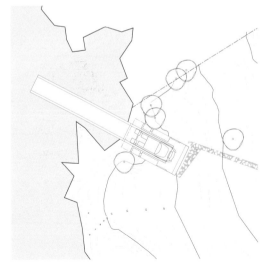

Boathouse site plan / Plan du site

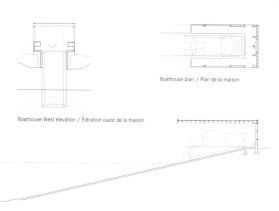

Boathouse plan / Plan de la maison

Boathouse West elevation / Élévation ouest de la maison

Boathouse section / Coupe de la maison

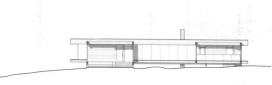

North elevation / Élévation nord

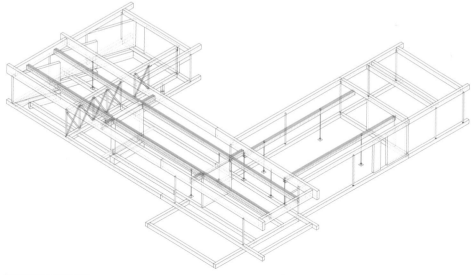

Axonometric view / Vue axonométrique

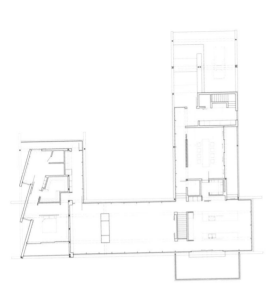

Main floor plan / Plan du niveau principal

Lower floor plan / Plan du niveau inférieur

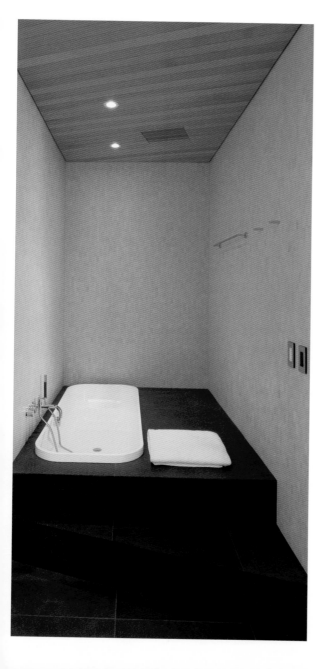

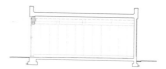

Garage long section / Coupe longitudinale du garage

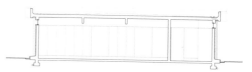

Garage cross section / Coupe transversale du garage

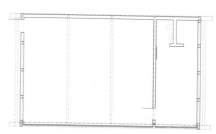

Garage main floor plan / Plan du garage au niveau principal

FAMILY HOUSE K
IN ZAGREB

ZAGREB, CROATIA
3LHD ARCHITECTS
www.3lhd.com | © Damir Fabijanic

The concept of the house is inspired by the shape of a conch. All living spaces are arranged around a central atrium. The facades and terraces are decorated with untreated teak wooden boards. The use of wooden panelling responds well to the spiral dynamic, creating an intimate and comfortable ambience.

Le concept de la maison s'inspire de la forme de la coquille d'un escargot. Tous les espaces de l'habitation se succèdent autour d'un atrium central. Les façades et les terrasses sont décorées avec des panneaux en teck non traité. L'utilisation de ces panneaux répond à la progression en spirale pour obtenir un endroit intime et confortable.

Das Konzept des Hauses wurde von der Schneckenform inspiriert. Alle Räume des Wohnhauses sind um ein zentrales Atrium herum angeordnet. Die Fassaden und Terrassen wurden mit Tafeln aus unbehandeltem Teakholz dekoriert. Der Gebrauch der Holzpaneele entspricht der Spiralform, um eine intime und komfortable Atmosphäre zu erhalten.

Het concept van dit huis is geïnspireerd op de vorm van een slakkenhuis. Alle ruimten van de woning liggen rondom een centraal gelegen atrium. De puien en terrassen zijn gedecoreerd met onbehandelde teakhouten platen. De gebruikte houten panelen volgen de geleidelijke spiraalvorm en gaan vervolgens over in een intieme en comfortabele ruimte.

El concepto de la casa se inspira en la forma de una concha de caracol. Todos los espacios de la vivienda se suceden y se construyen en torno a un atrio central. Las fachadas y terrazas están decoradas con tableros de madera de teca sin tratar. El uso de paneles de madera responde a la progresión en espiral para lograr un ambiente íntimo y confortable.

Il concetto della casa si ispira alla forma di una chiocciola. Tutti gli spazi dell'abitazione si succedono intorno all'atrio centrale. Le facciate e le terrazze sono decorate con tavole di legno tek non trattato. L'uso di pannelli di legno risponde alla progressione a spirale, per ottenere un ambiente intimo e confortevole.

O conceito desta casa inspira-se na forma de um caracol. Todos os espaços da casa se vão sucedendo em torno de um átrio central. As fachadas e terraços estão decorados com tábuas de madeira de teca sem tratamento. A aplicação de painéis de madeira obedece a uma progressão em espiral, para conseguir uma atmosfera de intimidade e conforto.

Husets koncept är inspirerat av formen på en snäcka. Alla utrymmena i bostaden följer efter varandra kring ett atrium i mitten. Fasader och terrasser är inredda med omålade brädor av teak. Användningen av träpaneler ska efterlikna en spiralrörelse, för att uppnå en intim och behaglig atmosfär.

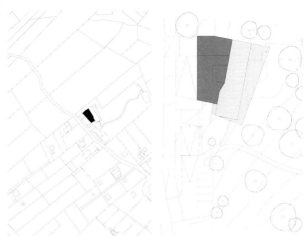

Site plans / Plans du site

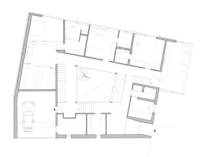

Upper level / Niveau supérieur

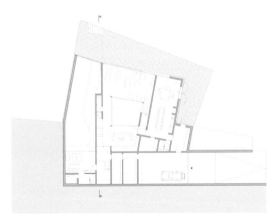

Lower level / Niveau inférieur

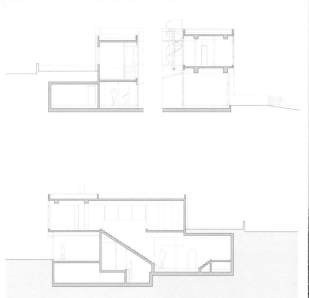

Sections / Coupes

ECOLOGIAL RESERVE
SINQUEFIELD HOUSE

OSAGE COUNTRY, MO, USA
BARTON PHELPS & ASSOCIATES
www.bpala.com | © Timothy Hursley

The project involves the renovation and expansion of a house built on top of a hill. A U-shaped
structure was created with one open side to take full advantage of light and to function as a
viewpoint over the surrounding natural environment. Wood is predominantly used as an integral
element for the exterior and interior.

Le projet consistait à transformer et agrandir une maison construite en haut d'une colline.
Afin de profiter au maximum de la lumière et de pouvoir admirer la nature environnante, une
structure en forme de U a été créée, avec un des côtés ouvert. L'utilisation du bois prédomine
à l'intérieur comme à l'extérieur.

Das Projekt besteht aus der Renovierung und Erweiterung eines Hauses, das auf dem Rücken
einer Anhöhe gebaut wurde. Es wurde eine Struktur in U-Form mit einer offenen Seite geschaffen,
um das Licht maximal zu nutzen und als Aussichtspunkt für die umgebende Natur zu fungieren.
Im Außen- und im Innenbereich dominiert die Verwendung von Holz als integrierendes Element.

Met dit ontwerp is een boven op een heuveltop gelegen huis verbouwd en uitgebreid. Om zo veel
mogelijk profijt te hebben van het licht en om een mooi uitzichtpunt te creëren op de omliggende
natuur, is een constructie gemaakt in een U-vorm, waarbij een van de zijden open is gelaten. Voor
de bouw van het exterieur en het interieur is hout het belangrijkste bestanddeel geweest.

El proyecto consiste en la reforma y ampliación de una casa construida en la cima de una colina.
Para aprovechar al máximo la luz y funcionar como mirador de la naturaleza que la rodea, se
creó una estructura en forma de U, con uno de sus lados abierto. En el exterior y en el interior
predomina el uso de la madera como elemento integrador.

Il progetto consiste nella ristrutturazione e ampliamento di una casa costruita in cima ad una
collina. Per sfruttare al massimo la luce e essere utilizzata come osservatorio della natura che la
circonda, è stata creata una struttura a forma di U, con uno dei lati aperti. All'esterno e all'interno
domina l'uso del legno come elemento integrante.

Este projeto consistiu na remodelação e ampliação de uma casa construída no alto de uma
colina. Para aproveitar ao máximo a luz e funcionar como miradouro sobre a natureza envolvente,
criou-se uma estrutura em forma de «U», com um dos lados aberto. Tanto no exterior como no
interior impera o uso da madeira como elemento integrante.

Projektet består av en renovering och utbyggnad av ett hus som är byggt på toppen av en
kulle. För att till fullo nyttja ljuset och fungera som en utsiktspunkt över naturen som omger
det, skapade man en struktur i formen av ett U med en sida som är öppen. På ut- och insidan
dominerar användning av trä som en integrerande del.

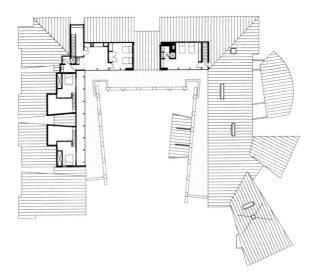

Second floor plan / Plan du second niveau

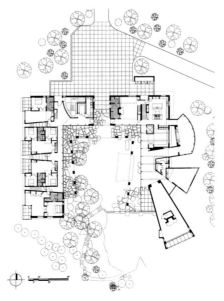

Ground floor plan / Plan du rez-de-chaussée

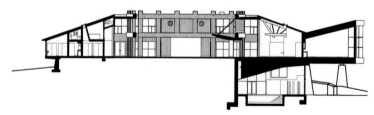

Sections / Coupes

SUMMERHOUSE
INSIDE OUT HVLER

PAPPER, NORWAY
REIULF RAMSTAD ARCHITECTS
www.reiulframstadarkitekter.no | © Roberto di Trani, Kim Müller

The house is located on top of a hill overlooking the sea. The particular design of the house allows a close interaction with the surrounding natural environment. Large glass windows allow all-round enjoyment of the scenery. The wooden facades are stained grey to integrate with nature.

L'habitation est située en haut d'une colline avec vue sur la mer. Le concept particulier de la maison offre une interaction étroite avec la nature environnante. Les grandes baies vitrées permettent de profiter du paysage dans tous les sens. Les façades en bois ont été teintes en gris pour s'intégrer dans la nature.

Das Wohnhaus liegt auf dem Gipfel einer Anhöhe mit Blick aufs Meer. Das spezielle Design des Hauses erlaubt eine enge Interaktion mit der umgebenden Natur. Die großen Glasfronten ermöglichen im wahrsten Sinne des Wortes den Genuss der Landschaft in vollen Zügen. Die Holzfassaden wurden grau eingefärbt, um sich in die Natur zu integrieren.

Deze woning ligt op de top van een heuvel en heeft uitzicht over zee. Dankzij het bijzondere ontwerp van het huis is er een nauwe interactie met de omringende natuur. Door de grote glazen ramen kan in alle opzichten uitgebreid worden genoten van het landschap. De houten puien zijn grijs geschilderd om integratie met de omliggende natuur te bewerkstelligen.

La vivienda se ubica en la cima de una colina con vistas al mar. El particular diseño de la casa permite una estrecha interacción con la naturaleza circundante. Los grandes ventanales de vidrio permiten la visualización en todos los sentidos del paisaje. Las fachadas de madera se tintan en gris para integrarse con la naturaleza.

L'abitazione è situata sulla cima di una collina con vista sul mare. Il particolare design della casa consente una stretta interazione con la natura circostante. I grandi finestroni di vetro consentono di godere del paesaggio in tutti i sensi. Le facciate di legno si dipingono di grigio per favorirne l'integrazione con la natura.

Esta casa está situada no alto de uma colina com vista para o mar. O seu design peculiar permite uma estreita interação com a natureza circundante. Os grandes janelões de vidro permitem desfrutar da paisagem em todas as direções. As fachadas vão-se tingindo de tons acinzentados para se integrarem com a natureza.

Bostaden ligger på toppen av en kulle med utsikt över havet. Den särskilda formgivningen av huset gör ett nära samspel med den omgivande naturen möjligt. De stora panoramafönstren gör det möjligt att njuta av landskapet i alla riktningar. Träfasaderna är målade i en grå ton för att passa in med och samspela med naturen.

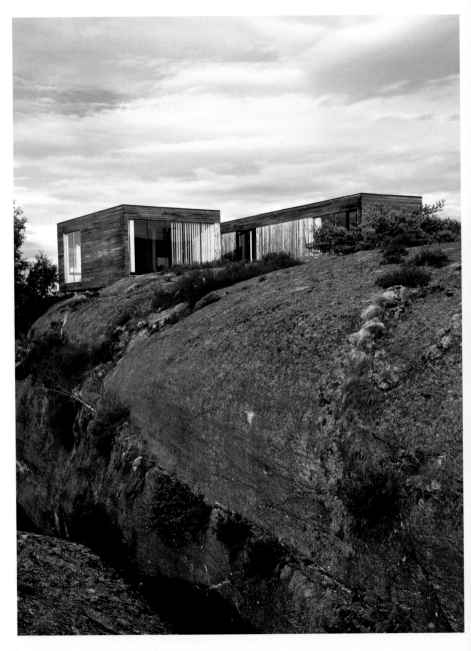

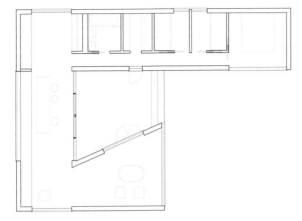

Plan

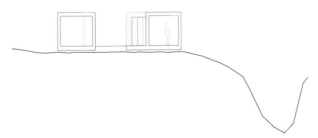

Section / Coupe

HOUSE OF STEEL AND WOOD
IN RANÓN

RANÓN, SPAIN
ECOSISTEMA URBANO
www.ecosistemaurbano.com | © Emilio P. Doiztua

The house is a contemporary reinterpretation of the local architecture of typical Asturian granaries. The use of wood was centred around the main frame and the enclosure. The enclosure consists of two types of wood: northern pine and Douglas fir. The double-height south facing conservatory is exceptional.

L'habitation est une réinterprétation moderne de l'architecture vernaculaire des greniers caractéristiques des Asturies. L'utilisation du bois s'est concentrée sur la structure principale et le bardage. Ce dernier se compose de deux types de bois : le sapin du Nord et le sapin de Douglas. On distingue la galerie vitrée à hauteur double, orientée vers le sud.

Das Wohnhaus ist eine zeitgenössische Neuinterpretation der einheimischen Architektur der typischen Kornkammern Asturiens. Die Verwendung von Holz steht bei der Hauptstruktur und den Außenwänden im Mittelpunkt . Die Außenwände setzen sich aus zwei Holzarten zusammen: nordische Kiefer und Douglas-Kiefer. Auffallend ist die verglaste Galerie in doppelter Höhe, die nach Süden ausgerichtet ist.

Met deze woning is de Spaanse bouwkunst van de typische 'hórreos' in Asturië op een nieuwe, moderne wijze geïnterpreteerd. Er is hout gebruikt voor met name het belangrijkste raamwerk en het sluitwerk. Voor het sluitwerk is gebruikgemaakt van twee soorten hout, van de noordse den en de douglasspar. Opvallend is de twee verdiepingen tellende galerij, met glazen puien die uitzicht bieden op het zuiden.

La vivienda es una reinterpretación contemporánea de la arquitectura vernácula de los típicos hórreos asturianos. El uso de la madera se ha centrado en la estructura principal y en el cerramiento. El cerramiento se compone de dos tipos de madera: el pino norte y el pino Douglas. Destaca la galería acristalada de doble altura orientada hacia el sur.

La casa è una reinterpretazione contemporanea dell'architettura vernacolare dei tipici *hórreos* (granai) asturiani. L'utilizzo del legno è stato concentrato nella struttura principale e nel tramezzo. Il tramezzo è costituito da due tipi di legno: il pino Nord e il pino Douglas. Spicca la veranda a vetro a doppia altezza orientata verso sud.

Esta casa é uma reinterpretação contemporânea da arquitetura vernacular dos espigueiros asturianos tradicionais. O uso da madeira encontra-se sobretudo na estrutura principal e nas paredes exteriores. Nestas últimas foram usados dois tipos de madeira: o pinho nórdico e o pinho Douglas. Destaca-se a galeria envidraçada de duplo pé-direito orientada para sul.

Bostaden är en nutida omtolkning av den inhemska arkitekturen för sädesmagasin i Asturien. Användningen av trä har framför allt gällt huvudbyggnaden och inhägnaden. Inhägnaden består av två typer av trä: tall och Douglasgran. Mest framträdande är ett glasförsett galleri med dubbel höjd i söderläge.

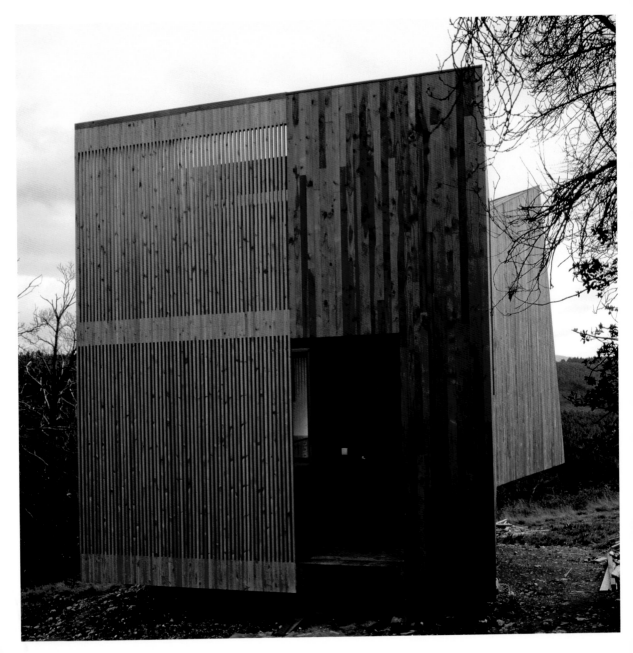

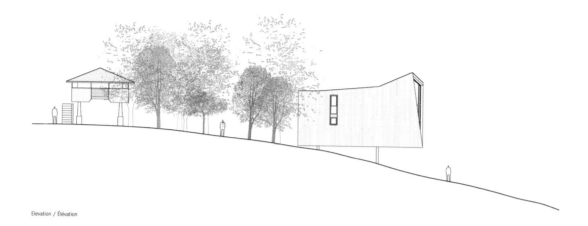

Elevation / Élévation

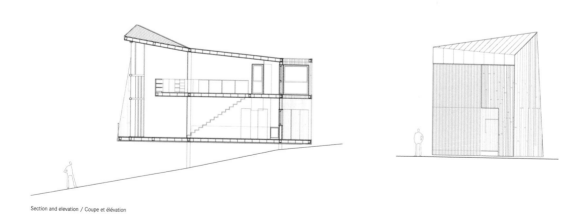

Section and elevation / Coupe et élévation

403

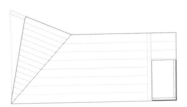

Roof plan / Plan du toit

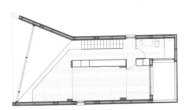

Ground floor plan / Plan du rez-de-chaussée

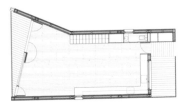

Entry plan / Plan de l'entrée

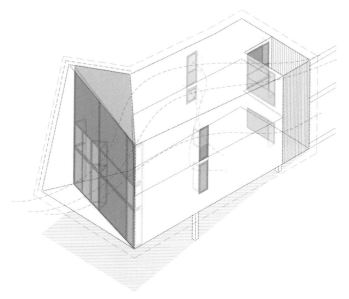

Bioclimatic scheme / Schéma bioclimatique

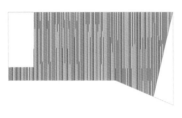

Elevations / Élévations

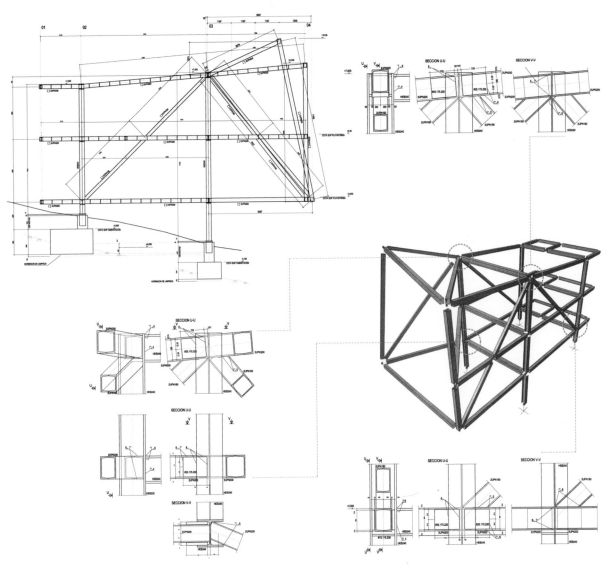

Details drawings of the structure / Dessins des détails de la structure

WOODEN HOUSE K
IN THE BLACK FOREST

GLATTEN, GERMANY
PARTNERUNDPARTNER ARCHITEKTEN
www.partnerundpartner.com | © Partnerundpartner architekten

The clients requested a contemporary house built of wood, providing maximum comfort and wellbeing within a limited budget. The architects created a house with a wooden frame constructed around a solid core of clay. The gable roof built from larch planks is impressive.

Les clients demandaient une maison moderne construite en bois, qui optimise confort et bien-être pour un budget limité. Les architectes ont créé une habitation familiale avec une structure en bois qui s'organise autour d'un noyau solide en argile. On distingue le toit à deux pentes construit avec des plaques de mélèze.

Die Kunden wünschten ein zeitgenössisches Haus aus Holz, das die Ansprüche an höchsten Komfort und Behaglichkeit bei geringem Budget erfüllen sollte. Die Architekten schufen ein Einfamilienhaus mit einer Holzstruktur, die sich um einen festen Lehmkern anordnet. Auffallend ist das Spitzdach aus Lerchenholztafeln.

De opdrachtgevers vroegen om een eigentijds houten huis dat ondanks beperkte financiële middelen toch zo veel mogelijk comfort en welbevinden zou bieden. De architecten ontwierpen een eengezinswoning met een houten raamwerk dat is gebouwd rondom een solide kern van klei. Opvallend is het dak dat is gemaakt van twee hellende larikshouten platen.

Los clientes demandaban una casa contemporánea construida en madera y que proporcionara el máximo confort y bienestar dentro de un presupuesto limitado. Los arquitectos crearon una vivienda unifamiliar con estructura de madera que se organiza alrededor de un núcleo sólido de arcilla. Destaca el techo a dos aguas construido con tablas de madera de alerce.

I clienti richiedevano una casa contemporanea costruita in legno e che offrisse il massimo comfort e agio con un budget limitato. Gli architetti hanno creato un'abitazione unifamiliare con struttura in legno che si dispone attorno a un nucleo solido di argilla. Spicca il tetto a due falde costruito con tavole di legno di larice.

Os clientes pretendiam uma casa contemporânea, construída em madeira e que proporcionasse o máximo conforto e bem-estar possíveis com um orçamento limitado. Os arquitetos criaram uma vivenda unifamiliar com estrutura de madeira organizada em volta de um núcleo sólido em barro. Destaca-se o telhado de duas águas construído com tábuas de madeira de larício.

Kunderna ville ha ett modernt hus byggt i trä med maximal bekvämlighet och trivsel inom en begränsad budget. Arkitekterna skapade ett enfamiljshus med en stomme av trä kring en fast kärna av lera. Mest framträdande är taket med plankor av lärkträ.

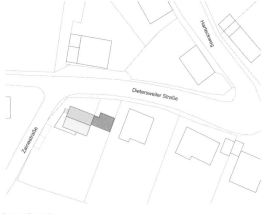

Site plan / Plan du site

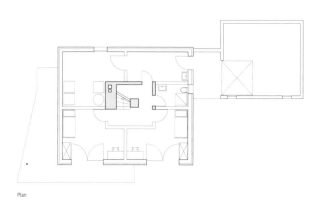

Plan

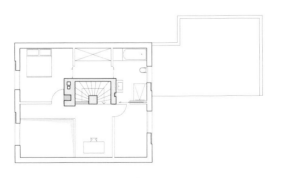

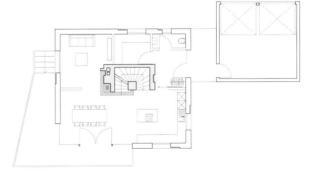

Plans

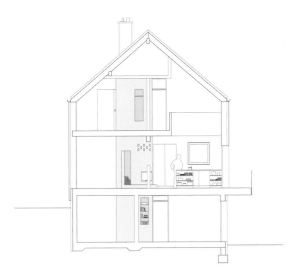

Section / Coupe

VORSÄSSHÜTTE
HOUSE S IN EGG

EGG, AUSTRIA
DIETRICH / UNTERTRIFALLER ARCHITEKTEN
www.dietrich.untertrifaller.com | © Ignacio Martínez

The house is situated on an alpine hill near Lake Constance. Although the design seems to follow the traditional alpine style of the region using larch wood for the surface of the facade, the structure has a more contemporary look. In the interior, as with the facade, wood has been used to provide a welcoming atmosphere.

La maison se situe sur une colline des Alpes, près du lac de Constance. Bien que le concept semble interpréter le style alpin traditionnel de la région, avec le revêtement de la façade en sapin, sa structure est plus moderne. À l'intérieur, comme pour la façade, le bois a été utilisé pour créer un environnement accueillant.

Das Haus liegt auf einem alpinen Bergrücken in der Nähe von Konstanz. Obwohl der Entwurf scheinbar den traditionellen alpinen Stil der Region interpretiert, mit einer Fassadenverkleidung aus Lerchenholz, ist die Struktur doch sehr zeitgemäß. Sowohl im Innenraum als auch für die Fassade, wurde Holz verwendet, um eine gemütliche Umgebung zu schaffen.

Dit huis staat op een berg in de buurt van het Meer van Konstanz (Duitsland). Hoewel het ontwerp veel lijkt op de traditionele bouw in deze bergstreek, doordat de voorgevel met larikshout is bekleed, straalt de constructie toch meer eigentijdsheid uit. Net als voor de façade is voor het interieur hout gebruikt om een warme uitstraling te creëren.

La casa se ubicó sobre una colina alpina cercana al lago Constanza. Aunque el diseño parece interpretar el tradicional estilo alpino de la región con el revestimiento de la fachada en madera de alerce, la estructura presenta más contemporaneidad. En el interior, como en la fachada, se ha utilizado la madera para lograr un ambiente cálido.

La casa è situata su una collina alpina vicina al lago di Costanza. Sebbene il design sembri interpretare lo stile alpino tradizionale della regione attraverso il rivestimento della facciata in legno di larice, la struttura presenta un carattere di maggiore contemporaneità. All'interno, come per la facciata, è stato utilizzato il legno per offrire un ambiente accogliente.

Esta casa fica situada numa montanha alpina, perto do lago de Constança. Embora o design pareça interpretar o estilo alpino tradicional da região, com a fachada revestida a madeira de larício, a sua estrutura é bem mais contemporânea. No interior, tal como na fachada, recorreu-se à madeira para criar um ambiente mais acolhedor.

Huset ligger på en höjd i Alperna nära Constanza. Även om formspråket verkar efterlikna regionens traditionella alpina stil, med lärkträ på fasaderna, är strukturen mer samtida. På insidan precis som på fasaden har trä använts för att ge en trivsam atmosfär.

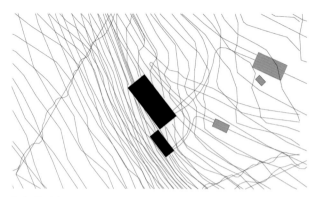

Site plan / Plan du site

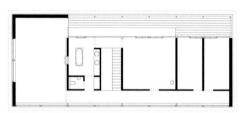

Second floor plan / Plan du second étage

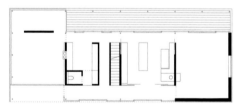

First floor plan / Plan du premier étage

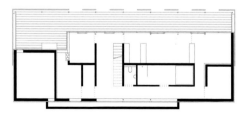

Ground floor plan / Plan du rez-de-chaussée

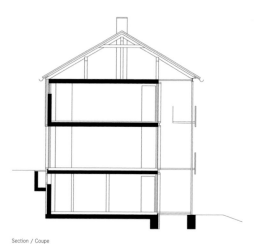

Section / Coupe

GÉOMÉTRIE BLEUE

HOLIDAY HOME

HAVRE-AUX-MAISONS, ÎLES DE LA MADELEINE, CANADA
**MARIE-CLAUDE HAMELIN, LOUKAS YIACOUVAKIS,
JULIE LAROUCHE / YIACOUVAKIS HAMELIN ARCHITECTES**
www.yh2architecture.com | © Jeff Mcnamara, Philippe Saharoff, Loukas Yiacouvakis

The architectural landscape of the Magdalen Islands is characterized by small, brightly coloured wooden structures. The remit of this project was to transform an existing house to provide a holiday home for the owners and their guests. Instead of expanding the existing house, they built a second building connected by an enclosed elevated cedar walkway.

Le paysage architectural des Îles de la Madeleine se caractérise par de petites structures de bois de couleurs vives. Ce projet consistait à transformer une maison pour créer une maison de vacances pour les propriétaires et leurs invités. Au lieu d'agrandir la partie existante, un deuxième bâtiment a été construit et relié au premier par une passerelle élevée en cèdre massif.

Die architektonische Landschaft der Magdalenen-Inseln wird geprägt von kleinen Holzstrukturen in leuchtenden Farben. Für dieses Projekt wurde ein bestehendes Haus transformiert, um ein Ferienhaus für die Eigentümer und ihre Gäste zu gestalten. Statt das bestehende Haus zu erweitern, wurde ein zweites Gebäude gebaut, das über einen hoch gelegenen, geschlossenen Steg aus Zedernholz mit dem ersten Haus verbunden ist.

Het bouwkundige landschap van de Magdalena-eilanden kenmerkt zich door kleine houten gebouwen in levendige kleuren. Dit ontwerp kwam tot stand met de verandering van een bestaand huis, zodat de eigenaren en hun gasten het in gebruik konden nemen als vakantiewoning. In plaats van het bestaande huis uit te breiden, is een tweede gebouw gemaakt dat met het eerste in verbinding staat door middel van een verhoogde passerelle van onvervalst cederhout.

El paisaje arquitectónico de las islas de la Magdalena se caracteriza por sus pequeñas estructuras de madera de colores vivos. En este proyecto se transformó una casa existente para crear una casa de vacaciones para los propietarios y sus invitados. En lugar de ampliar la existente se construyó un segundo edificio unido mediante una pasarela cerrada y elevada de cedro.

Il paesaggio architettonico delle isole della Madeleine è caratterizzato da piccole strutture di legno dai colori vivi. Questo progetto consisteva nel trasformare una casa esistente per dare vita a una casa di vacanza per i proprietari e gli invitati. Invece che ampliare quella esistente è stato costruito un secondo edificio collegato tramite una passerella rialzata e chiusa in cedro.

A paisagem arquitetônica das ilhas da Madalena é caracterizada por pequenas estruturas de madeira de cores vivas. Este projeto consistiu em transformar uma casa existente, para ser utilizada como casa de férias pelos proprietários e pelos seus convidados. Em vez de ampliar o já existente, construiu-se um segundo edifício, ligado ao primeiro por um passadiço sobrelevado e fechado em madeira de cedro.

Det arkitektoniska landskapet Îles de la Madeleine kännetecknas av små bjärt färgade träkonstruktioner. Detta projekt bestod i omvandla ett befintligt hus för att ge liv åt ett fritidshus för ägarna och deras gäster. I stället för att göra det befintliga större skapade man en andra byggnad som förenades via en gångbro av cederträ.

LA CASITA
PLAY HOUSE

NUMMI PUSULA, FINLAND
BACH ARQUITECTES
www.bacharquitectes.com | © Tiia Ettala

The house is based on a section of a simple structure, which is repeated in two equal modules pointing in opposite directions. Spruce was used for the frame, floors, walls and roof. One part of the house was painted with vertical white stripes, and the remainder was left untreated so as to acquire a greyish hue over time.

La maison repose sur une structure simple qui se répète sur deux modules identiques orientés dans des sens opposés. Pour celle-ci, on a utilisé du sapin ainsi que pour les sols, les murs et la toiture. Une partie de l'habitation a été peinte avec des lignes verticales blanches et le reste a été laissé tel quel afin d'acquérir au fil du temps un ton grisâtre.

Das Haus basiert auf einem Bereich mit einer einfachen Struktur, die sich in zwei gleichen Modulen wiederholt, welche in zwei entgegengesetzten Richtungen ausgerichtet sind. Für die Struktur, die Böden, die Wände und das Dach wurde Tannenholz verwendet. Ein Teil des Wohnhauses wurde mit weißen, vertikalen Linien gestrichen und der Rest des Holzes wurde nicht behandelt, so dass es mit der Zeit einen gräulichen Ton annimmt.

De basis van dit huis bestaat uit een eenvoudige constructie die zich herhaalt in twee gelijke modules die onderling in tegengestelde richting staan. Voor het raamwerk, de vloeren, de wanden en het dak is sparrenhout gebruikt. Een deel van de zitkamer is beschilderd met witte banen, de rest van het hout is onbehandeld zodat het met de tijd een grijzige tint krijgt.

La casa se basa en una sección de estructura simple que se repite en dos módulos iguales orientados en direcciones opuestas. Para la estructura, los suelos, las paredes y la cubierta se utilizó madera de abeto. Una parte de la vivienda se pintó con franjas blancas verticales y el resto se dejó sin tratar para que fuera tomando con el paso del tiempo un tono grisáceo.

La casa si basa su una sezione dalla struttura semplice che si ripete in due moduli uguali orientati in direzioni opposte. Per la struttura, i pavimenti, le pareti e il tetto è stato utilizzato legno di abete. Una parte dell'abitazione è stata dipinta a strisce bianche verticali, e il resto è stato lasciato non trattato in modo che acquisisse una tonalità grigiastra col passare del tempo.

A casa baseia-se numa seção estruturalmente simples que se repete em dois módulos iguais orientados em direções opostas. Para a estrutura, pavimentos, paredes e teto utilizou-se madeira de abeto. Uma parte da casa foi pintada com listas brancas verticais, ficando o restante por tratar, para que fosse adquirindo um tom acinzentado com o passar do tempo.

Huset bygger på en sektion av en enkel struktur som upprepas i två lika moduler riktade i motsatta riktningar. Granvirke användes för stomme, golv, väggar och tak. En del av huset målades med vertikala vita ränder och resten lämnades obehandlat så att det får en grå ton med tidens gång.

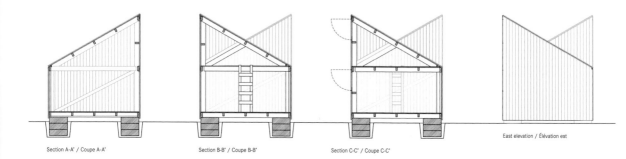

Section A-A' / Coupe A-A'   Section B-B' / Coupe B-B'   Section C-C' / Coupe C-C'   East elevation / Élévation est

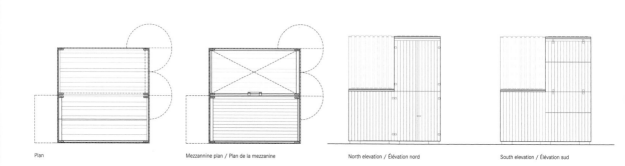

Plan   Mezzannine plan / Plan de la mezzanine   North elevation / Élévation nord   South elevation / Élévation sud

RESIDENTIAL EXTERIORS

EXTÉRIEURS RÉSIDENTIELS

AUSSENBEREICHE VON WOHNHÄUSERN

EXTERIEURS

EXTERIORES RESIDENCIALES

ESTERNI AD USO ABITATIVO

EXTERIORES RESIDENCIAIS

BOSTADSEXTERIÖRER

SUMMER RETREAT
IN FUGLEVIK

FUGLEVIK, NORWAY
REIULF RAMSTAD ARCHITECTS
www.reiulframstadarkitekter.no | © Reiulf Ramstad Architects

The summer house was designed around the concept of a single viewpoint, which means that the house opens out onto the landscape in one single direction. The exterior and interior of the building were constructed entirely of wood. The wooden slats provide rhythm and harmony to the entire architecture of the building.

La résidence d'été a été conçue sur la base du concept de point de vue unique. Autrement dit, la maison s'ouvre au paysage dans une seule direction. La construction a été entièrement réalisée en bois, tant à l'extérieur qu'à l'intérieur. Les lattes de bois apportent rythme et harmonie à l'ensemble architectural.

Das Sommerhaus wurde auf der Basis des Konzepts entwickelt, dass nur ein einziger Standpunkt besteht. Das bedeutet, dass das Haus sich nur in eine einzige Richtung zur Natur hin öffnet. Der Bau wurde vollständig in Holz realisiert, sowohl Außen als auch Innen. Die Holzlatten sorgen für Rhythmus und Harmonie der architektonischen Einheit.

Deze zomerwoning is ontworpen vanuit het concept van een enkel gezichtspunt. Het huis staat slechts in een enkele richting open naar het landschap. Zowel het exterieur als het interieur zijn volledig uit hout opgetrokken. Door het gebruik van houten latten ontstaan ritme en harmonie in het bouwkundige geheel.

La vivienda de verano se diseñó en torno al concepto de un único punto de vista, lo que significa que la casa se abre hacia el paisaje en una sola dirección. La construcción se realizó integramente en madera tanto en el exterior como en el interior. Los listones de madera aportan ritmo y armonía en el conjunto arquitectónico.

La residenza estiva è stata progettata attorno al concetto di un punto di vista unico, il che significa che la casa si apre verso il paesaggio in un'unica direzione. La costruzione è stata realizzata completamente in legno, sia all'esterno sia all'interno. I listoni di legno apportano ritmo e armonia all'insieme architettonico.

Esta residência de verão foi desenhada com base no conceito de um único ponto de vista, o que significa que toda a casa se abre para a paisagem numa única direção. A construção foi executada exclusivamente em madeira, tanto no exterior quanto no interior. As tábuas de madeira conferem ritmo e harmonia a todo o conjunto arquitetônico.

Sommarbostaden utformades kring idén om en enda utsiktspunkt, vilket innebär att huset endast öppnar sig mot landskapet i en enda riktning. Byggnaden utfördes helt i trä, såväl på in- som utsida. Trälisterna tillför rytm och harmoni till den arkitektoniska helheten.

Elevations / Élévations

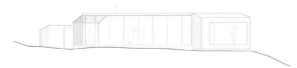

Elevations / Élévations

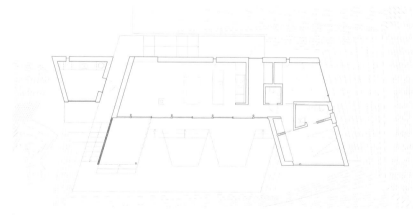

Plan

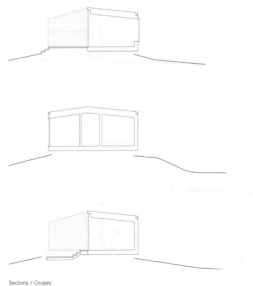

Sections / Coupes

SINGLE-FAMILY
VILLA RBDVD

STOCKHOLM, SWEDEN
RB ARKITEKTUR
www.rbarkitektur.se | © Ulrika Ekblomr

The house follows the Swedish tradition of wooden, single-family homes with standardized prefabricated construction and architectural expression. The house features a simple rectangular structure and clearly defined areas with interrelated internal subdivisions.

L'habitation répond à la tradition suédoise des maisons unifamiliales en bois, où les éléments préfabriqués sont soumis à des normes, tant pour la construction que pour l'expression architecturale. La maison se caractérise par une structure simple de forme rectangulaire et par une définition claire des espaces où les subdivisions internes sont reliées entre elles.

Das Wohnhaus entspricht der schwedischen Tradition der Einfamilienhäuser aus Holz, bei denen Fertigteile sowohl für den Bau als auch für den architektonischen Ausdruck standardisiert sind. Das Haus zeichnet sich durch eine einfache, rechteckige Struktur aus und hat eine klare Definition der Räume, in denen die internen Unterteilungen miteinander in Beziehung treten.

Deze woning sluit aan bij de Zweedse traditie van houten eengezinswoningen waarvan de geprefabriceerde delen, zowel in de uitvoering als wat betreft de architectonische expressie, gestandaardiseerd zijn. Dit huis kenmerkt zich door zijn eenvoudige structuur, een rechthoekige vorm en een duidelijke afbakening van de ruimten waarvan de interne onderverdelingen weer onderling met elkaar verbonden zijn.

La vivienda responde a la tradición sueca de las casas unifamiliares de madera donde los prefabricados está estandarizados tanto en la construcción como en la expresión arquitectónica. La casa se caracteriza por una estructura simple de forma rectangular y una definición de espacios clara donde las subdivisiones internas se relacionan entre sí.

L'abitazione risponde alla tradizione svedese di case unifamiliari in legno, dove i prefabbricati risultano standardizzati sia nella costruzione sia nell'espressione architettonica. La casa è caratterizzata da una struttura semplice a forma rettangolare e da una chiara definizione di spazi in cui le suddivisioni interne sono in rapporto tra loro.

Esta vivenda obedece à tradição sueca das casas unifamiliares de madeira, onde os pré-fabricados estão estandardizados, tanto na construção como na expressão arquitetônica. A casa caraterisa-se por uma estrutura simples de forma retangular e uma clara definição de espaços em que as subdivisões internas se relacionam entre si.

Bostaden stämmer in på den svenska traditionen för enfamiljshus av trä, där de prefabricerade är standardiserade i konstruktion och arkitektoniskt uttryck. Huset kännetecknas av en enkel rektangulär konstruktion och en tydlig definition av utrymmen där de inre skiljeväggarna hänger ihop.

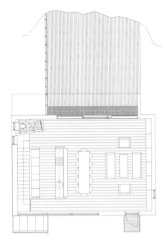

Upper level / Niveau supérieur

Lower level / Niveau inférieur

East elevation / Élévation est

North elevation / Élévation nord

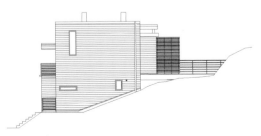

West elevation / Élévation ouest

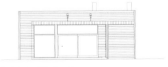

South elevation / Élévation sud

Section / Coupe

THREE-CHILD
FAMILY DWELLING S. IN W.

FLANDERS REGION, BELGIUM
BURO II & ARCHI + I, ROESELARE
www.b2ai.com | © Kris Vandamme

The design was influenced by the location and natural environment surrounding the house. The residence was oriented in a north-south direction in order to accommodate an access area to the west and a garden with private pool to the east. Wood has been used to create divisions between spaces and between the concrete platforms.

Le concept a été influencé par la situation et la nature qui entoure l'habitation. La résidence a été orientée dans un axe nord-sud pour abriter une zone d'accès à l'ouest et un jardin oriental avec piscine privée. Le bois a été utilisé pour séparer les espaces et les plates-formes en béton.

Das Design wurde durch die Lage und die Natur, welche das Wohnhaus umgibt, beeinflusst. Das Wohnhaus hat eine nordsüdliche Ausrichtung, um einen Zugangsbereich nach Westen, mit einem orientalischen Garten und privatem Schwimmbad zu ermöglichen. Das Holz wurde als Trennmaterial zwischen den Räumen und den Betonplattformen eingesetzt.

Dit ontwerp is beïnvloed door de ligging en de natuur rondom de woning. Het gebouw volgt een lijn in de richting van noord naar zuid. Het toegangsgebied ligt op het westen en aan de oostzijde is een tuin met privézwembad. Om de ruimten van elkaar te scheiden en tussen de betonnen balkons is gebruikgemaakt van hout.

El diseño fue influenciado por el sitio de ubicación y la naturaleza que rodea la vivienda. La residencia se orientó en una línea norte-sur para albergar una zona de acceso al oeste y un jardín oriental con piscina privada. La madera se ha utilizado como material divisorio entre espacios y como paramento entre las plataformas de hormigón.

Il progetto fu influenzato dall'ubicazione e dalla natura che circonda l'edificio. La residenza fu orientata secondo una linea nord-sud per ospitare un'area di accesso a ovest e un giardino orientale con piscina privata. Il legno è stato utilizzato come materiale di separazione tra spazi e solette di cemento.

O design deste projeto foi influenciado pela localização e pelo ambiente natural envolvente. A casa foi orientada no sentido norte-sul, de modo a albergar uma zona de entrada a oeste e um jardim oriental com piscina privada. A madeira foi utilizada como material de divisão entre espaços e entre as plataformas de betão.

Formen har influerats av platsen och naturen som omger huset. Villan placerades efter en nord-sydlig linje för att ge plats åt ett område med ingång från väster och en trädgård med privat pool i öster. Trä har använts på ett sätt som skapar effekten av uppdelade utrymmen.

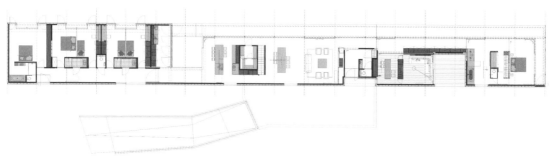

Plan

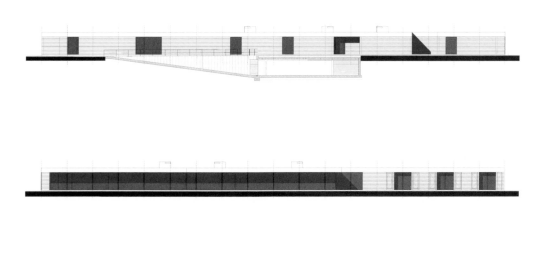

Elevations and sections / Élévations et coupes

DECK HOUSE
IN AUSTIN

AUSTIN, TX, USA
MIRÓ RIVERA ARCHITECTS
www.mirorivera.com | © Miró Rivera Architects

The structure, located in a very steep terrain boasting a spectacular view of the Texas Hill Country, is a holiday home annexed to the principal residence without direct access. An outstanding feature is the large outdoor platform which arises from between the different spaces that compose the house.

La structure, située sur un terrain très escarpé qui offre une vue spectaculaire sur le Hill Country du Texas, est une résidence de vacances qui s'est ajoutée à la résidence principale sans accès direct. Les différents espaces qui constituent la maison font ressortir la grande plate-forme extérieure, entièrement construite en bois.

Der Bau liegt auf einem sehr abschüssigen Gelände, von dem man eine spektakuläre Aussicht auf Hill Country in Texas hat. Es ist ein Ferienhaus, das man an das Haupthaus angefügt hat, ohne dass es einen direkten Zugang gibt. Von den unterschiedlichen Räumen, die das Haus bilden, sticht die äußere Plattform ab, die riesige Ausmaße hat und vollständig aus Holz gebaut wurde.

Deze constructie is gebouwd op een bijzonder steil terrein vanwaar kan worden genoten van een spectaculair uitzicht over de Hill Country in Texas. Dit vakantiehuis werd toegevoegd aan het hoofdhuis zonder dat het daarmee direct in verbinding staat. Van de verschillende ruimten waaruit het huis bestaat, valt vooral het enorme platform op aan de buitenzijde, dat volledig uit hout is geconstrueerd.

La estructura, situada en un terreno muy escarpado donde se puede contemplar- una vista espectacular del Hill Country de Texas, es una casa de vacaciones que se añadió a la residencia principal sin acceso directo. De entre los diferentes espacios que componen la casa, destaca la plataforma exterior de grandes dimensiones y construida totalmente en madera.

La struttura, situata su di un terreno molto scosceso da cui è possibile godere di una vista spettacolare dell'Hill Country del Texas, è una casa di vacanza che è stata aggiunta all'abitazione principale senza accesso diretto. Tra i vari spazi che compongono la casa, spicca la piattaforma esterna di grandi dimensioni costruita interamente in legno.

Esta estrutura, situada num terreno muito escarpado, de onde se pode desfrutar de uma vista espetacular sobre o Hill Country do Texas, é uma casa de férias que se acrescentou à residência principal, sem acesso direto. Entre os diferentes espaços que compõem a casa destaca-se a plataforma exterior de grandes dimensões, totalmente construída em madeira.

Strukturen, som är belägen i en mycket brant terräng varifrån man kan njuta av en spektakulär utsikt över Hill Country i Texas, är ett semesterboende som byggdes ihop med huvudbyggnaden utan egen ingång. Av de olika utrymmena som utgör huset står den yttre stora plattformen, byggd helt i trä, i en klass för sig.

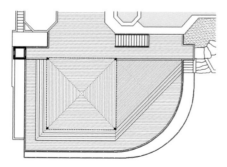

Upper level / Niveau supérieur

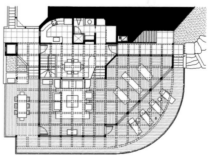

Lower level / Niveau inférieur

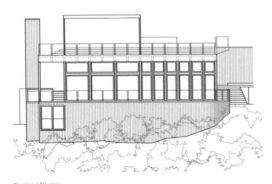

Elevation / Élévation

T SPACE
IN DUTCHESS COUNTY

DUTCHESS COUNTY, NY, USA
STEVEN HOLL ARCHITECTS
www.stevenholl.com| © Susan Wides

Near the main house, which dates from 1952, a small T-shaped building was created. The outstanding feature of the project, in addition to its wooden frame, is its positioning on top of nine columns and elevations, creating the impression that it is actually floating. Wood also dominates the interior, allowing for the creation of skylights.

Un petit bâtiment en forme de « T » a été créé à côté de l'habitation principale datant de 1952. La particularité du projet, outre sa construction principale en bois, réside dans sa disposition sur neuf colonnes et élévations qui alimentent l'impression de flotter à la surface. L'intérieur est également dominé par le bois, qui permet la création de lucarnes.

In der Nähe des Haupthauses, das aus dem Jahre 1952 stammt, wurde ein kleines Gebäude in T-Form errichtet. Das Besondere an diesem Projekt ist, abgesehen von der Hauptkonstruktion aus Holz,, dass das Haus auf neun Säulen und Erhebungen aufliegt, was den Eindruck vermittelt, als schwebe man über der Oberfläche. Auch im Innenraum dominiert das Holz, in dem Oberlichter eingebaut werden konnten.

Vlakbij het hoofdgebouw van 1952 is een gebouwtje neergezet in de vorm van een T. Het is een bijzondere constructie, niet alleen omdat het vooral uit hout is opgetrokken, maar ook omdat gebouw rust op negen pijlers en verhogingen waardoor het lijkt alsof het boven de oppervlakte zweeft. Ook het interieur bestaat voornamelijk uit hout, waarin verschillende dakvensters zijn gemaakt.

Cerca de la vivienda principal que data de 1952, se creó una pequeña edificación en forma de T. La singularidad del proyecto, además de su construcción principal en madera, es su asentamiento sobre nueve columnas y elevaciones que la hace parecer flotar sobre la superficie. En el interior también predomina la madera, que permite la apertura de claraboyas.

Vicino all'abitazione principale, datata 1952, è stato creato un piccolo edificio a forma di T. La particolarità del progetto, oltre alla sua costruzione principale in legno, è la sua installazione su nove colonne e rialzamenti che alimentano l'idea di apparente galleggiamento sulla superficie. Anche all'interno domina il legno, che permette la creazione di lucernari.

Perto da casa principal, que data de 1952, foi criado um pequeno edifício em forma de T. A singularidade do projeto, para além da utilização predominante da madeira, é o fato de estar sobrelevado, assente em nove colunas, dando a ideia de estar flutuando acima do solo. No interior também domina a madeira, que permite a criação de claraboias.

Nära huvudbyggnaden, från 1952, skapade man en liten byggnad i formen av ett T. Det unika med projektet, förutom dess huvudbyggnad i trä, är sättningen på nio pelare och upphöjningar som när känslan av att verka sväva ovanför ytan. Även på insidan är trä dominerande, där det är möjligt att skapa takfönster.

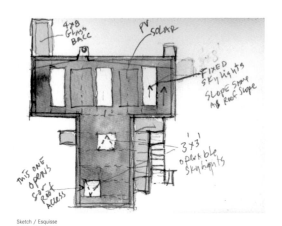

Sketch / Esquisse

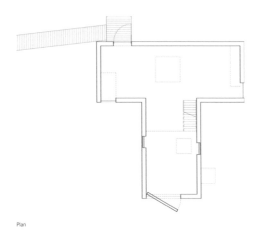

Plan

FLAP TERRACE RIEGEL
IN HANNOVER

HANNOVER, GERMANY
MARTIN DESPANG ARCHITEKTEN
www.despangarchitekten.de | © Despang Architekten

The terrace is a new take on space as an outdoor place to relax and unwind. The focus of the project was the creation of a wooden structure that serves as cover and that evolves into a lattice wall, reaching up to a cantilevered roof canopy. The wood is of thermic origin and is supported by zinc-coated steel sections.

La terrasse est devenue une nouvelle manière de prendre en compte l'espace extérieur comme lieu de détente et de repos. Le projet se concentrait sur la création d'une structure en bois qui fait office de recouvrement, évolue sur un mur en treillis et avance sur un pare-soleil en saillie. Le bois est d'origine thermique et repose sur des poutrelles en acier recouvertes de zinc.

Die Terrasse ist eine Neubetrachtung des Raumes als Entspannungs- und Ruheort unter freiem Himmel. Das Hauptaugenmerk des Projekts lag auf der Erschaffung einer Holzstruktur, die als Dachkonstruktion dient und in eine Fachwerkwand übergeht, um später in einem Vorbau zu enden. Das Holz hat thermische Eigenschaften und stützt sich auf verzinkte Stahlprofile.

Voor dit terras is met een nieuwe blik gekeken naar de ruimte als plaats in de openlucht om te ontspannen en uit te rusten. Het uitgangspunt voor het ontwerp was het creëren van een houten constructie die dienstdoet als een dak dat geleidelijk overgaat in een wand van latwerk en verder doorloopt in een vooruitstekende overkapping. Het thermisch gemodificeerde hout steunt op stalen profielen die zijn bekleed met zink.

La terraza es una reconsideración del espacio como un lugar al aire libre para relajarse y descansar. El enfoque del proyecto fue la creación de una estructura de madera que funciona como cubierta que evoluciona y avanza en un muro de celosía y avanza en un toldo de techo en voladizo. La madera es de origen térmico y se apoya en perfiles de acero recubiertos de zinc.

La terrazza è una riconsiderazione dello spazio come luogo all'aria aperta per rilassarsi e riposare. Il fulcro del progetto fu la creazione di una struttura di legno che funge da copertura e che si sviluppa in un muro reticolato per proseguire in una tenda da soffitto a sbalzo. Il legno è di origine termica e poggia su profili di acciaio zincato.

Este terraço é uma reformulação do espaço como local ao ar livre destinado ao relaxamento e ao descanso. O projeto centrou-se sobretudo na criação de uma estrutura de madeira que funciona como cobertura, evoluindo depois para uma parede gradeada e avançando finalmente para formar um telheiro. A madeira é termorretificada e suportada por perfis de aço revestidos a zinco.

Terrassen är en omprövning av utrymmet som en plats i det fria för att slappna av och vila. I fokus för projektet var skapandet av en struktur av trä som fungerar som ett skyddstak och förändras gradvis till ett spjälverk och utvecklas till ett utsprång som soltak. Virket är värmebevarande och vilar på stålspjälor överdragna med zink.

YETA
RIFUGIO CAMALEONTE

VAL DI SELLA, ITALY
LAB ZERO
www.lab-zero.com | © Lab Zero

Yeta is a structure used for different purposes: a room with a view, a research laboratory, a mountain retreat, a place for observing the natural environment, a cottage, a seating area and a meditation space. The design is based on the piles of tree trunks seen in alpine pastures and forests. Inside, there are a kitchen and a bathroom.

Yeta est une structure utilisée à des fins différentes : maison avec vue, laboratoire de recherche, refuge de montagne, lieu d'observation de la nature, maison de campagne, zone de repos et espace de méditation. Le concept se base sur les piles de troncs d'arbres des pâturages alpins et des bois. L'intérieur abrite une cuisine et une baignoire.

Yeta ist eine Struktur, die für verschiedene Zwecke verwendet wird: Zimmer mit Aussicht, Forschungslabor, Berghütte, Observationsort für die natürliche Umgebung, Landhaus, Ruhezone und Meditationsort. Das Design basiert auf den Holzstapeln der Baumstämme auf der Alm und in den Wäldern. Der Innenraum beherbergt eine Küche und ein Badezimmer.

De Yeta wordt gebruikt voor verschillende doeleinden: als kamer met uitzicht, onderzoekslaboratorium, berghut, natuurobservatiepost, buitenhuis, rustplaats en meditatieruimte. Het ontwerp bestaat uit een constructie van op elkaar gestapelde boomstammen en is gebouwd op bergweiden en in bossen. Binnenin bevinden zich een keuken en een badkamer.

Yeta es una estructura usada para diferentes fines: habitación con vistas, laboratorio de investigación, refugio de montaña, lugar de observación de entornos naturales, casa de campo, zona de descanso y espacio de meditación. El diseño se basa en las pilas de troncos de los árboles sobre los pastos alpinos y los bosques. El interior alberga una cocina y un baño.

Yeta è una struttura utilizzata con differenti finalità: stanze con viste, laboratorio di ricerca, rifugio di montagna, sito di osservazione di ambienti naturali, casa di campagna, area di riposo e spazio per la meditazione. Il design si basa sulle pile di tronchi d'alberi sui pascoli alpini e i boschi. L'interno ospita cucina e bagno.

A Yeta é uma estrutura que pode ser usada para diversos fins: quarto com vista, laboratório de investigação, abrigo de montanha, local de observação do maio natural, casa de campo, zona de descanso e espaço de meditação. O seu design baseia-se nas pilhas de troncos de troncos de árvore habituais nas pastagens e florestas alpinas. O interior está equipado com cozinha e banheiro.

Yeta är en struktur som används för olika ändamål: rum med utsikt, undersökningslaboratorium, härbärge i bergen, utkiksplats i naturen, lantställe, område för vila och meditationsplats. Formen bygger på travarna av trädstammar på de alpinska betesmarkerna och skogen. I byggnaden finns kök och badrum.

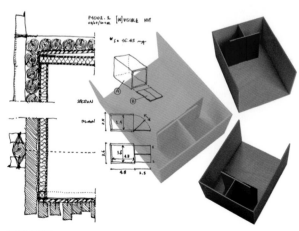

Scheme / Schémas

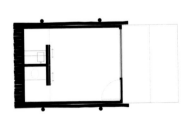

Plan

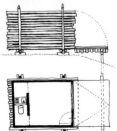

Concept sketch / Esquisse conceptuelle

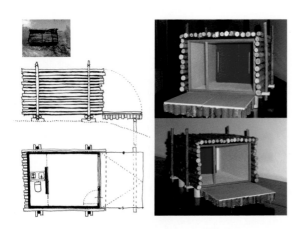

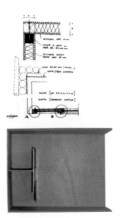

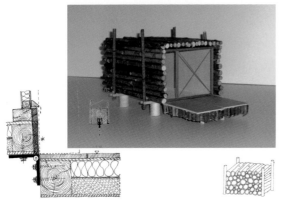

Schemes / Schémas